Anonymous

Seventh Annual Meeting and Banquet of the Pennsylvania Scotch-Irish Society

At the Hotel Bellevue, Philadelphia

Anonymous

Seventh Annual Meeting and Banquet of the Pennsylvania Scotch-Irish Society
At the Hotel Bellevue, Philadelphia

ISBN/EAN:

Printed in Europe, USA, Canada, Australia, Japan

Cover: Foto ©ninafisch / pixelio.de

More available books at **www.hansebooks.com**

SEVENTH ANNUAL MEETING

AND

BANQUET

OF THE

PENNSYLVANIA SCOTCH-IRISH SOCIETY,

AT THE

HOTEL BELLEVUE, PHILADELPHIA,

FEBRUARY 13th, 1896.

PHILADELPHIA:

ALLEN, LANE & SCOTT'S PRINTING HOUSE,

1211-13 Clover Street.

1897.

SEVENTH ANNUAL MEETING

AND

BANQUET

OF THE

PENNSYLVANIA
SCOTCH-IRISH SOCIETY,

AT THE

HOTEL BELLEVUE, PHILADELPHIA,

FEBRUARY 13th, 1896.

———◆———

PHILADELPHIA:
ALLEN, LANE & SCOTT'S PRINTING HOUSE,
1211-13 Clover Street.
1897.

142915

OFFICERS.

PRESIDENT,
HON. JAMES A. LOGAN.

FIRST VICE-PRESIDENT,
MR. WILLIAM RIGHTER FISHER.

SECOND VICE-PRESIDENT,
JUSTICE HENRY W. WILLIAMS.

SECRETARY AND TREASURER,
MR. CHARLES L. McKEEHAN.

DIRECTORS AND MEMBERS OF COUNCIL:

MR. A. K. McCLURE,	HON. JAMES GAY GORDON,
MR. T. ELLIOTT PATTERSON,	MR. W. W. PORTER,
REV. J. S. MACINTOSH, D. D.,	REV. S. D. McCONNELL, D. D.,
HON. R. M. HENDERSON,	MR. ROBERT PITCAIRN,
MR. J. BAYARD HENRY,	MR. JAMES POLLOCK,
MR. SAMUEL F. HOUSTON,	MR. C. STUART PATTERSON,
REV. HENRY C. McCOOK, D. D.,	COL. JOHN CASSELS.

COMMITTEES.

ON ADMISSION OF MEMBERS:

WM. RIGHTER FISHER, *Chairman*,	ROBERT PITCAIRN,
W. W. PORTER,	J. BAYARD HENRY,
C. S. PATTERSON,	C. L. McKEEHAN.

FINANCE:
THE OFFICERS OF THE SOCIETY.

ON ENTERTAINMENTS:

HENRY W. WILLIAMS, *Chairman*,	T. ELLIOTT PATTERSON,
A. K. McCLURE,	JAMES POLLOCK,
JOHN CASSELS.	

HISTORY AND ARCHIVES:

HENRY C. McCOOK, *Chairman*,	HON. JAMES GAY GORDON,
SAMUEL F. HOUSTON,	HON. R. M. HENDERSON.

DIAGRAM OF THE BANQU

	Hon. Benton McMillen.	Hon. J. B. McCreary.	Hon. Josiah Patterson.	Hon. John M. Allen.	Hon. R. G. Cousins.	Hon. Jos. C. Ferguson.	W. W. Porter.	Rev. Dr. McConnell.	Bishop Thompson.
	X	X	X	X	X	X	X	X	X

Left		Center (3)		Right
Rev. Alex. Henry.	X			
Prof. J. C. Rice.	X	X	J. M. Barnett.	John McIlhenny.	X
Jos. Cousans.	X	X	T. H. Patterson.	John D. McIlhenny.	X
John H. Merrill.	X	X	J. H. Chestnut.	Oliver Bradin.	X
E. D. Faries.	X	X	George Hay.	John W. Woodside.	X
Geo. B. Bonnell.	X	X	James Hay.	Hon. R. L. Wright.	X
J. D. Campbell.	X	X	H. Holmes.	J. F. Magee.	X
Wm. R. Fisher.	X	X	G. McKeown.	G. G. Mercer.	X
J. Bayard Henry.	X	X	M. W. McAlarney.	Rev. Jas. D. Steele.	X
Rev. Wm. A. Patton.	X	X	Dr. Egle.	Dr. James MacAlister.	X
					X
Rev. Dr. J. H. Munro.	X	X	J. A. McDowell.		
				W. P. Sanderson.	X
F. J. Geiger.	X	X	Chas. T. Schoen.		

James Pollock.

ГCH-IRISH SOCIETY.

ABLE, FEBRUARY 13th, 1896.

Hon. J. A. Logan.   Senator Lindsay.   C. S. Patterson.   Geo. V. Massey.   Justice Williams.   Col. A. K. McClure.   Hon. J. C. Burrows.   Hon. E. S. Stuart.   John H. Converse.

x   x   x   x   x   x   x   x   x

			x Chas. L. McKeehan.
x Jas. A. Stranahan.	Rev. D. O. Moffitt.	x	x Rev. O. B. McCurdy.
x Hon. S. J. M. McCarrell.	John Furguson.	x	x T. E. Patterson.
x R. S. Reed.	H. S. P. Nichols.	x	x W. H. McCrea.
x W. S. Wallace.	J. F. Magee.	x	x John S. Lloyd.
x John C. Harvey.	J. R. Young.	x	x John Graham.
x S. G. Scott.	**1**	x	x W. N. Heulings.
x Wm. H. Scott.	Hon. W. H. Armstrong.	x	x Robt. McMeen.
x Dr. Hugh Pitcairn.	J. B. Kinley.	x	x W. J. Latta.
x W. W. Hanna.	Dr. Wm. Thomson.	x	x Wm. A. Patton.
x R. A. Patton.	John P. Green.	x	x A. B. Rorke.
x Rev. Dr. Duncan.	Geo. F. Huff.	x	x L. S. Bent.
		x	

Col. John Cassels.

SEVENTH ANNUAL MEETING.

———⊕———

THE seventh annual meeting and banquet of the
Pennsylvania Scotch-Irish Society was held at the
Hotel Bellevue, Philadelphia, February 13th, 1896,
Rev. Henry C. McCook, D. D., in the chair.

The report of William Righter Fisher, tempora-
rily acting as Secretary and Treasurer in place of
C. W. McKeehan, deceased, was presented and approved.

On recommendation of the Council it was unanimously resolved that Article V. of the Constitution
and By-Laws be amended so as to read as follows :—

" At each annual meeting there shall be elected a President,
a First and Second Vice-President, a Treasurer, a Secretary,
and twelve Directors, but the same person may be both Secretary and Treasurer.

" They shall enter upon office on the 1st of March next
succeeding, and shall serve for one year and until their successors are chosen. The officers and Directors, together with the
ex-Presidents of the Society, shall constitute the Council. Of
the Council there shall be four standing committees.

" 1. On Admission, consisting of four Directors, the Secretary, and the First Vice-President.

" 2. On Finance, consisting of the officers of the Society.

" 3. On Entertainments, consisting of the Second Vice-
President and four Directors.

" 4. On History and Archives, consisting of four Directors."

Upon the nomination of Hon. Edwin S. Stuart the following officers and Board of Directors were elected to serve for the ensuing year :—

President, Hon. JAMES A. LOGAN.
First Vice-President, WILLIAM RIGHTER FISHER.
Second Vice-President, JUSTICE HENRY W. WILLIAMS.
Board of Directors and Members of Council:

COL. A. K. McCLURE,	MR. JAMES POLLOCK,
MR. C. STUART PATTERSON,	MR. W. W. PORTER,
HON. R. M. HENDERSON,	REV. S. D. McCONNELL, D.D.,
REV. J. S. MACINTOSH, D.D.,	COL. JOHN CASSELS,
MR. T. ELLIOTT PATTERSON,	MR. ROBERT PITCAIRN,
MR. J. BAYARD HENRY,	HON. JAMES GAY GORDON,
MR. SAMUEL F. HOUSTON,	REV. HENRY C. McCOOK, D.D.

On motion, it was resolved that the election of a permanent Secretary and Treasurer be referred to the Council for their action, and that Mr. Fisher be requested to continue to serve the Society in that capacity until the place shall be permanently filled.

On motion, the business meeting was then adjourned, and the company proceeded to the banqueting room, where the President, Rev. Dr. Henry C. McCook, took the chair.

Rev. Alexander Henry invoked the Divine blessing.

During the progress of the dinner Rev. Henry C. McCook, D.D., President, arose and spoke as follows :—

GENTLEMEN :—One purpose of our existence as an organization is to keep green the memory of the distinguished persons who have the honor of being our ancestors, and to do what we may, through the influence of this Society, on each meeting thereof, to set some one feature of the honorable service of our ancestors prominently before guests and members. You may remember that this was one of the favorite ideas of our late Secretary. Instead of giving an address to-night, as has been the custom of our Presidents in vacating office, it has seemed to me that the best service I could render would be to contribute an historical paper, and the Committee has fixed upon this particular point in the order for the introduction of this paper. I have chosen for my subject "Stephen Collins Foster, the Scotch-Irish bard and balladist." The address will be interspersed with a few of his favorite songs, and the Council has had printed and placed before you this souvenir book of words that you may intelligently follow the trained quartette of singers who have been engaged for the occasion. Perhaps some of you will feel like joining in the songs.

Pennsylvania's Scotch-Irish Bard and Balladist, Stephen C. Foster.

There is one department of activity in which the mental vigor and quenchless energy of the Scotch-Irish race has but scant representation. However we may account for it, the fact is that Ulster men have rarely broken forth into song. The minstrels of the early era of their origin have not transmitted their genius through their Ulstrian line of descent. By some inexplicable sport of destiny it seems to have been shunted upon other ethnic side tracks.

It is more difficult to understand this fact in view of the genius of our Scotch ancestors for song. There are Fergusson, Buchanan, James Bailie, Horatio Bonar, George MacDonald, Sir Walter Scott, the Wizard of the North, and " a boon them a' " Robbie Burns, whose matchless ballads voiced so sweetly Scotland's poetic genius, and are ringing still among the heathered hills of Caledonia and wherever her sons wander and dwell.

At all events, Ulster Americans can point to one scion of their race in whose breast the old bardic fire broke forth into a flame that is burning still in the hearts of Americans. The songs of Stephen C. Foster marked an important era in the development of the American ballad.

8

If there is any spot in America that by especial eminence may be held to be the head centre of Scotch-Irish habitatio n and influence it is that hilly tongue of land that lies at the forks of the Monongahela and Allegheny Rivers, commonly known as Pittsburgh. There Stephen Collins Foster was born, July 4th, 1826, in a suburb known as Lawrenceville, which now forms part of the Sixteenth Ward of the city. At that time there was no dwelling, except a farm house or two and the Brick Tavern on Two-Mile Run, between Grant Street and the place of Foster's birth. The house in which he was born was a white cottage, with a broad central door with rounded top and narrow side windows, leading into a spacious hall that parted the building into equal halves.

It stood upon a slight elevation overlooking the Allegheny River, and commanding an unobstructed view of that stream and the beautiful hills that rolled beyond. Back of the house and descending to Two-Mile Run, and stretching thence to the Monongahela River, was an almost unbroken forest, divided by what was then called the "Old Road," cut by General Forbes' army when it marched to the capture of Fort Duquesne. Just in front lay the island upon which General Washington, then a hardy young surveyor, was cast from his raft at the close of a dark December day in 1753. Over the ground on which the white cottage afterward stood Washington pursued his way when he made his historic visit to Queen Allequippa's wigwam.

It was the custom of Major William B. Foster, Stephen's father, to celebrate the Fourth of July by a "bowery dinner," in modern phrase "a lawn party." On that eventful anniversary of Independence, when Thomas Jefferson and John Adams died, a company of two hundred men and women, culled from the best society of the vicinity, were gathered upon the grounds and under the shade of the wide-spreading oaks upon Mr. Foster's estate. Tables were spread upon the green underneath the trees.

Intermingled with the dark coats of civilians and the bright gowns of the women guests were the uniforms of a number of officers from the arsenal just over the hill from the grove and from the barracks where Old Fort Pitt stood. Pittsburgh was then an important point for supplying government posts in the West with men and munitions of war, and thus the soldier element formed relatively an important part of the social life of Pittsburgh.

At twelve o'clock, when the guests were being gathered to the tables, according to the custom then prevailing, the arsenal guns thundered forth their national salute. Several field pieces that had been placed in Foster's grove answered the salute, and the great hills around echoed with a mighty uproar.

It was on this gala day, in the midst of this rejoicing and noise, that the future singer insisted upon lifting up the first wail of his infant voice. It is sometimes inconvenient—to others at least—to be ahead of one's time. We may well imagine the uneasiness with which the gentlemanly host greeted the guests who had come at his bidding, and how great was his relief when his bowery dinner was ended, amidst the congratulations of friends that another son had been born into his household. Small wonder, indeed, if those who trod the paths and roads along the hill slopes to their various homes that day had caught the spirit of ancient oracles and augurs, and predicted for the child whose birth had been attended by such martial and patriotic scenes a future of stirring activity in camp and field or in the halls of State. Yet nothing could have been further from the facts, for the ambition of the man was as far removed from the prognostications of his birth as is the Star of Bethlehem from the fires of Moloch.

His Ancestors.

Here we may pause to point out Foster's claims to a place among the distinguished sons of the Scotch-Irish stock. About the year 1728 Alexander Foster removed from Londonderry, Ireland, to America. In 1740 we find him settled in Little Britain Township, Lancaster County, Pa. His son, James Foster, of this pure Scotch-Irish stock, was married to

Anne Barclay, of the same unmixed blood. This young
wedded couple removed to Berkeley County, Va., and, with
the patriotic and belligerent instincts of his race, James took
part in the Revolutionary War as a member of the Virginia
Line, and was present at the closing scene, the surrender at
Yorktown.

Shortly afterward he removed to Washington County, Pennsylvania, and settled in the vicinity of Canonsburg. He was
one of the six first trustees of Canonsburg Academy, estab-
lished in 1791, out of which subsequently grew Jefferson
College. His son, William Barclay Foster, was born in Virginia, September 7th, 1779, and afterwards migrated with his
parents to Washington County. He studied in the famous
Log School of Dr. John McMillan, the pioneer teacher and
preacher of the West. In 1796 he removed to Pittsburgh, and
was associated in business with Major Ebenezer Denny, and in
1807 was married to Eliza Clayland Tomlinson, whose ancestors had removed from the West Riding of Yorkshire to the
eastern shore of Maryland.

These were the parents of Stephen C. Foster. The father
was a sterling patriot, and proved his fidelity by his deeds. In
1814 he was appointed Commissary and Quartermaster of the
United States Army. At that time the Government was well
nigh bankrupt and without credit, and Major Foster sacrificed
the most of his fortune and, with his own money, supplied
the Northwestern Army under "Old Tippecanoe," General
William Henry Harrison, and Jackson's army at New Orleans.
He loaded the steamer "Enterprise" with supplies and munitions of war for Jackson's army, and dispatched her from
Pittsburgh under the command of Capt. H. M. Shreve, on the
15th of December, 1814.

The boat arrived at New Orleans the 15th of January, 1815,
just in time to allow the skipper to serve at the sixth gun in
the American batteries, and contribute to the one great land
victory of the war of 1812 which helped somewhat to brighten
the unfortunate record of that conflict with Great Britain.

Thus we see that there was good blood in Stephen, with a
strong Scotch-Irish tone, and enough of the softer blood of

Yorkshire to temper and perhaps to tune his nature, and give it the cast and bias which set this scion of a warrior stock among the sweet singers of the land.

STEPHEN'S HOME LIFE.

These parents gave to Stephen a happy, cultured, and pious home life, and one of his strongest characteristics was his passionate love of home and his loyal devotion to his parents. His mother was a beautiful woman, wise, gentle, and loving. She was brave and consistent in her dealing with her large family, and firm in the administration of discipline and the guidance of her children. Her influence over her home was a continual blessing. She was a woman of large culture, a reader in all lines of useful literature, but was especially versed in the Holy Scriptures, and a faithful follower of its precepts. This trait Stephen inherited, for he had strong religious convictions, and an unquestioning, childlike faith in the Scriptures and in his Redeemer. He was a constant and interested reader of the Old and New Testaments, and delighted to discourse upon them with those who sympathized with him. However, he never could be drawn into controversy, which he avoided by the simple expression of his belief in the Bible, or by a quotation that expressed the limit of human ability, such as, " Who by searching can find out God ?"

Stephen's father was of Presbyterian ancestry and faith, but his mother was a devout member of the Protestant Episcopal Church ; and although not a member of that venerable communion himself, Stephen's sympathies and preferences were for his mother's church. It was largely due to the influence of this strong and saintly character that the Foster household was a peaceful and happy home.

ORIGIN OF SOME OF FOSTER'S SONGS.

Stephen's tender love of his home and his parents directly or indirectly influenced the form of some of his most beautiful and popular songs. In the Spring of 1852 he and his wife and brothers, with a party of friends and neighbors, took a trip to New Orleans, down the Ohio and Mississippi Rivers, on a steamboat belonging to his elder brother, Capt. Dunning McNair Foster. At that time his father was well advanced in life, and was an invalid confined to his room. After the return of the party from New Orleans, where Stephen obtained his first and most complete observation of negro life in the far South, he wrote the song, " Massa's in de Cold, Cold Ground." This seems to have been suggested by thoughts of his father's failing years, and of the obtruding shade and sorrow of his approaching death.

In the following lines especially he expressed the sympathy and grief stirred within him as he heard the feeble voice of his venerable parent asking aid of the devoted wife and children who waited around his couch.

> " When Autumn leaves were falling,
> When the days were cold,
> 'Twas hard to hear Ole Massa callin'
> Kayse he was so weak and old."

The best and most popular of Foster's songs, perhaps, is " Old Folks at Home," more generally known as " Suwanee River." This ballad was written in 1851. It was the product of peculiar circumstances. He had gone to New York to live, tempted by flattering assurances from his publishers, which were largely realized. He first had lodgings on Greene Street, and afterwards kept house in Hoboken. But no consideration of pecuniary advantage could recompense Stephen for the pain of separation from his home. He suddenly broke up housekeeping and returned to Pittsburgh and to the arms of that mother whom he loved more than life. While she lived he never left home again. It was out of this experience that he evolved the ballad which is known and sung wherever the English tongue is heard, and which the Swedish nightingale, Jenny Lind, once declared to be the sweetest ballad ever written in any language.

The incidents connected with the writing of " Old Folks at Home " are worthy of notice. A casual reader of the ballad would think that the writer must have been upon the Suwanee River, as many of you have been in these latter days, and that the words that flowed from his pen were tempered by a thorough knowledge of negro life in the embowered cottages and cabins of the Land of Flowers. On the contrary, Foster never saw Florida. While the piece was humming in his head he sought for the name of some Southern stream that would rhyme in melodiously with his thought and theme. He consulted a brother, now the Hon. Morrison Foster, who still lives in the vicinity of Pittsburgh, and this gentleman took down an atlas, and after searching along the Southern belt of States found thereon a small stream in the western portion of Florida called Suwanee River.

That is it! Just what the bard wanted! And so the mellifluous name flowed into the composer's song, and thus that little stream won its immortality. The song was written in the Summer of 1851, and was first rendered by the noted Christy Minstrels of that time, whose leader, E. P. Christy, paid Foster $500 for the right to use it.

How many men have heard it or sung it when far away from scenes of early life and from the paternal home, and have felt their hearts stirred and melted by memories of the past, and drawn with quenchless yearning towards that " dearest spot on earth—Home, Sweet Home ! "

It is to the credit of the home builders of our Republic, to the sweet and strong home influence of mothers, wives, and sisters, and equally creditable to the domestic nature of American men, who are habitually " true to the kindred points of Heaven and home," that the greatest ballads of home in the English tongue, " Home, Sweet Home " and " Old Folks at Home," were written by two Americans, John Howard Payne and Stephen Collins Foster. (Applause.) Still as we sing and hear sung these strains we feel the unutterable yearning of homesickness.

> " All the world grows sad and dreary,
> Everywhere I roam ;
> Oh, darkies, how my heart grows weary,
> Far from the old folks at home ! "

" Old Dog Tray," which was written in 1853, was one of Foster's most popular songs. It is not written in the negro vernacular, but has the peculiar elements of the negro melodies. It was suggested by the writer's friendly relation to a setter, presented to him by his friend, Mr. Matthew J. Stewart. This dog was a most intelligent and affectionate fellow, and delighted in the society of his master and his master's friends. He would lie on the floor while these gentlemen were engaged in conversation, and gaze from one to another as they severally took up the conversation, as though he were listening with as keen interest and understanding as his human friends.

Foster was a lover of nature in all its varied moods ; outdoor life had great charms for him, and he was never lonely when he could go forth into the woods, or along the banks of the river, or through the meadows in companionship with his dog, and in close and sympathetic fellowship with the works of the Divine Creator. This was his habit from childhood, and often when he should have been at his books he was finding more agreeable, and perhaps more helpful and wholesome, companionship in communion with nature.

" Old Dog Tray " has struck a responsive chord in many breasts. Who of us has not had a dog friend in boyhood days, if not in manhood's years? Mrs. Harriet Beecher Stowe. once remarked, " that since she had learned more of men, she had a higher respect and affection for her dogs." (Laughter.) No doubt that is an exaggeration ; nevertheless, it has its side of truth. Certainly there are men in plenty, whose society would have for us no charms at all as compared with the silent, intelligent, devoted friendship and companionship of some of the dogs we have owned and loved.

Foster introduces the same sentiment that pervades " Old Dog Tray " into one of the most touching of his plantation melodies : " O Boys, Carry Me 'long."

> " Farewell to de hills, de meadows covered with green,
>   Old Brindle Boss, an' de old gray hoss,
> All beaten, broken, and lean.
>   Farewell to de dog dat always followed me 'round,
>   Old Sancho 'll wail an' drop his tail
>   When I am under de ground."

We wonder, did the bard share the hopes of those who believe, with the aborigines of our own continent, that the dog and horse, with whom man has shared the conflicts and comforts of life, will share with him the felicities of the Happy Hunting Ground? There is much to be said in favor of animal immortality. Certainly, at least, if the eternal fitness of things and the principles of justice are to prevail beyond the limits of our terrestrial horizon, these dumb creatures, the domestic animals, who have been man's helpers in every step of his advancement toward higher civilization, may still be permitted to share with him the immortal conclusions of his imperishable being. (Applause.) Be that as it may, our memories and hearts alike respond gratefully to Foster's sentiments :—

> "Old Dog Tray's ever faithful,
>   Grief cannot drive him away ;
> He's gentle, he is kind, I'll never, never find
>   A better friend than old Dog Tray.

> "When thoughts recall the past
> His eyes are on me cast ;
>   I know that he feels what my breaking heart would say.
> Although he cannot speak,
> I'll vainly, vainly seek
>   A better friend than old Dog Tray."

"Old Kentucky Home."

One of the sweetest and one of the best of Foster's plantation melodies is "Old Kentucky Home." Indeed, there are those who find in it greater attraction and merit than even in "Old Folks at Home." Both the words and the music appeal to the tenderest feelings of the human heart. They strike a chord of longing for home, which so frequently and effectively Foster has touched, and from which he has evoked his most pathetic and popular strains.

Like "Old Folks at Home" and "Massa's in de Cold, Cold Ground," the ballad known as "Old Dog Tray" gets much of its pathos and hold upon the heart from the manner in which the home sentiment is interwoven therewith. Mark, for example, the first verse :—

> "The morn of life is past, and ev'ning comes at last,
> It brings me a dream of a once happy day,
> Of merry forms I've seen, upon the village green,
> Sporting with my old Dog Tray."

As one sings this verse, does he not see coming out of memory the shadowy forms of the boys and the girls that he loved in childhood, and with whom he played? They troop across his fancy, and bring with them recollections, affections, and incidents that awaken the smile and the tear, and mellow the heart into that strong tenderness which only comes with thoughts of "the days of Auld Lang Syne," with its "auld acquentance" which ne'er can be forgot.

"My Old Kentucky Home" was written in Cincinnati while Foster was residing there, making an effort, which proved to be futile, to adopt a business life. His brother, Capt. Dunning McNair Foster, was then engaged in business, and it was while he was a resident in that city that he made his first successful efforts in writing music and songs, and gave them out for publication. Across the Ohio River on the Kentucky side, about two miles from Bardstown, lived a relative, Judge Rowan. His residence was known as Federal Hill, and Foster often visited it. He loved the family and loved the place. This appears to have suggested to him the words of "Old Kentucky Home," at least the title thereof. The picture which he gives in his song perfectly presents the life on a plantation in the border States, as many of us remember it in the days " befoh the wah."

We see the bright sunshine of the American atmosphere gilding the mansion and the cabin, the ripening corn, the blooming meadows; the birds making music all the day; the cute, wee pickaninnies rolling like kittens on the naked floor, often *in puris naturalibus*, one of the prettiest sights that a man has ever seen, your speaker thinks. We see the full moon shining upon the negro quarters ; we hear the tum, tum of the banjo, and the mellow voices of the colored folk as they sing their songs rise through the silent night. Far away on the distant hills the baying of dogs, the shouting of men, and perhaps the sound of the horn are heard where the darkey is hunting the 'possum and the coon. Then, with that pathos of which Foster is a master, the scene changes. Old age has come. The pleasures of life are gone. We behold the vanishing of all these happy scenes, and the sweetness and hope of those happy hearts, as the curtain falls and the lights are turned down, and all is ended.

> " They hunt no more for de 'possum and de coon
> On the meadow, the hill, and the shore,
> They sing no more by the glimmer of the moon
> On the bench by the old cabin door.

> " The day goes by like a shadow o'er the heart,
> With sorrow where all was delight ;
> The time has come when the darkies have to part,
> Then, my old Kentucky home, good night."

THE CHARACTER OF FOSTER'S MUSIC.

It is the fashion of the cultured musicians to look upon Foster's music slightingly. His works have little or no place in the historical records of musical achievements. The masters of melody look down from their lofty height upon them as unworthy of notice. Olympian melodies are for themselves alone. The negro melodist, the singer of folk songs, what is he compared to these demigods of the celestial heights? Yet Foster was not ignorant of the most scientific music. He was thoroughly acquainted with the works of Mozart, Beethoven, and Weber, and these were his constant themes. He loved to play and hear played the works of these great masters. He made an especial study of harmonies as well, and was by no means ignorant of what musical specialists regard as the only worthy forms in which to give melodious utterance to human sentiment.

Nevertheless, the people, at least, have not been convinced that the masters are right. With them Foster's songs have a higher place and value than the most artistic music, because they belong to nature. They are born of the deepest feelings of the human heart. They well out of the primary rocks, the very core of human sentiment. They reach depths of feeling and heights of fancy which no mere artificial music can attain. They lie, like the poems of Burns, close up to the broad bosom of our Mother Nature. They have been adopted by the people, for they were born out of the homely, yet divinely natural, sentiments which are the basal structure of the human heart. The man who produces songs like these, though he may not be an expert from the standpoint of a technical composer and performer, is nevertheless a genius, and is entitled to recognition as a sovereign in his own sphere.

We have no word to say derogatory of the masters. In their place they are supreme, and are to be honored and heard. Foster belongs to the same order indeed, but to a different genus ; and we are here only expressing the popular protest against that narrowness of vision with which men from the altitudes of scientific music survey all that seems to be beneath them. The musical laymen at least think that their altitude should have given them a wider horizon and a clearer view. But whether the masters applaud or disapprove, our Scotch-Irish bard and balladist from his own particular point of vantage shall, no doubt, keep his hold upon the hearts of men in the future as he has done in the past. Songs like " Old Folks at Home," " Old Kentucky Home," and " Old Dog Tray " never can perish while man retains the constitution which God has given him.

The verses of Foster are of unequal merit from a literary standpoint, though none of them can be given a high place simply as poetry. His negro songs are perhaps the best. But whatever defects or merits may be allowed, one must admit that the words have been wedded to the music with masterly felicity. Of course, such " catch songs " as " Nelly Bly " and " Oh, Susanna ! " must be counted among the ephemera of the current time ; yet even these have renewed their youth in selections of college songs, in nearly all of which they have a place.

ANTI-SLAVERY INFLUENCE.

There is one point in connection with the history of Foster's productions which, as far as I know, has never been publicly referred to, and which certainly has never been generally considered. They had a great influence in moulding the political future of our Republic. We all know the saying of the song maker, " Let me make the ballads of a nation and I care not who makes its laws." Sentiment is one of the mightiest forces in shaping human destiny ; and sentiment lives and finds utterance in popular songs. It can hardly be questioned that Foster's negro melodies had as much to do as any other instrumentality in preparing the way for emancipation and the events which attended it. •

It would be impossible to estimate the influence which his negro melodies exercised, throughout the whole country, in bringing the thoughts and feelings of the people into strong sympathy with the colored race as men and women. The idea of their being chattels was simply sung away by the sweet and sympathetic strains of Foster and his associates and imitators in the field of negro minstrelsy.

The slaves' essential humanity, their common inheritance of all the tenderest ties and loves of life, were presented in such an inimitable, irresistible, and insinuating way that opposition was disarmed and the heart of the nation was captured. Before men knew it, before the slaveholders had suspected it, the work was done. Negro minstrelsy undermined the system of chattel bondage, and made it impossible for slavery to maintain its position in this continent. (Applause.)

It tempered largely the feeling of the slaveholders themselves, and strengthened the strong affections and convictions of that large and better element among them which was always mindful of the human feeling, aspirations, and necessities of their bondmen, and sought to make the best of the social conditions into which they had been born. It prompted and encouraged them to sweeten the bitter cup of slavery with the milk of human kindness. (Applause.) This was especially true throughout the border States, where domestic slavery took upon itself, more largely than in the Gulf States, the form of a domestic institution, in which servants were regarded less as chattels than as human friends and helpers and members of the common household.

I have heard these negro melodies of Foster and others sung in the very heart of slave-holding districts by the ladies of the plantation mansion, while men, young and old, stood around listening to or sharing in the music and the singing. The servants heard the songs and caught the words and music, and Foster's melodies might have been heard ringing, not only in the mansion of the white master, but in the humble cabin of the black slave, in the days before the Rebellion.

Imagine, if you can, what must have been the influence under such circumstances of the singing of such a verse as this:—

> "Oh, carry me 'long, dere's no more trouble for me,
> I'se gwine to roam in a happy home,
> Where all de niggas am free."

Or such a verse as this:—

> "The head must bow, and the back will have to bend,
> Wherever the darkey may go ;
> A few more days and the trouble all will end
> In the field where the sugar canes grow.
> A few more days for to tote the weary load,
> No matter, 'twill never be light;
> A few more days will we totter on the road,
> Then, my old Kentucky home, good night!"

What must have been the effect, though the singers were not conscious thereof, of the popular use of such a song as B. R. Hanby's "Darling Nelly Gray"?

> "One night I went to see her, but 'she's gone!' the neighbors say,
> The white man bound her with his chain ;
> They have taken her to Georgia for to wear her life away,
> As she toils in the cotton and the cane.

CHORUS.

> "Oh! my darling Nelly Gray, they have taken you away,
> And I'll never see my darling any more,
> I am sitting by the river and I'm weeping all the day,
> For you've gone from the old Kentucky shore."

I have heard that song sung in a slave-holding community in a border State wherein, but a few days before, I had seen the breaking up of a large plantation and the sale of individuals at public auction, the most of them purchased by the dreaded trader for the distant and more Southern section. They

who sung and heard the same seemed oblivious of the fact that
they were uttering in song the condemnation of the social
system under which they had been bred, and that they were
surely establishing within their own hearts, or at least the
hearts of their children, a sentiment of comradeship, of brother-
hood, of equality in human rights to the fundamental loves,
sympathies, and sentiments of humanity, before which inevit-
ably the chains of the bondman must melt away.

No doubt Foster's songs helped to create the sentiment
which united the Northern States against the establishment
of a Republic whose " corner stone should be slavery." But it
is just possible for us to conjecture that the same sweet yet
potent influences might have so wrought upon the hearts of
the slaveholders themselves that they would have been led in
the end to emancipate their own slaves. However we specu-
late upon this we can hardly deny, speaking from an historical
standpoint, that Stephen Foster was the instrument, perhaps
the unconscious instrument, of summoning forth one of the
mightiest forces that brought about the political revolution
that resulted in the emancipation of American slaves.

In politics Foster, like his father, was an old-fashioned Jackson Democrat (applause), as was my own father, and indeed
myself (renewed applause), until I got my eyes opened.
(Laughter and applause.) But during the war against the
Rebellion he was a devoted patriot, and his zeal for the preservation of the Republic was expressed in several Union songs.
Among the best known are: " We are Coming, Father Abra-
ham;" " We've a Million in the Field;" and " For the Dear
Old Flag I Die."

FOSTER'S EDUCATION AND MUSICAL DEVELOPMENT.

As a boy Stephen attended the school of " Old John Kelly,"
in Allegheny, where so many Pittsburghers received their
early instruction. At the age of thirteen he visited Towanda,
the home of his elder brother, William B. Foster, then State
engineer, and afterwards a vice-president of the Pennsylvania Railroad. While a member of his brother's family he

attended college at Athens, Pa., and here his first musical composition was made public. It was a quartette for flutes, known as the "Tioga Waltz," and which was performed at the College Commencement in 1840.

At the age of fifteen Foster returned to his native city, and shortly thereafter entered Jefferson College at Canonsburg. He is described at this time as a slender, dark-eyed lad, self-poised, gentle, and thoughtful. He had few close friendships, and was more devoted to music and nature than to the dead languages. Nevertheless, he acquired a fair knowledge of Latin, and was a good French and German scholar.

He left Jefferson College without graduating, and after a brief stay at home in Pittsburgh made the effort to engage in business in Cincinnati, which has already been alluded to. After two years spent in his brother's office as a bookkeeper he abandoned business and gave full play to his musical genius. While in Cincinnati he met Mr. W. C. Peters, a leading music dealer and publisher of that city, to whom he presented the manuscript of "Old Uncle Ned" and "Oh, Susanna," which proved a valuable gift to the publisher, for the two songs are said to have realized $10,000.

At the age of twenty-one we again find Foster in Pittsburgh, devoting himself wholly to song writing, having made an arrangement with the New York house of Firth, Pond & Co. to bring out all his compositions. In 1849 he wrote "Nelly was a Lady," and a number of works of lesser merit.

The most fertile period of Foster's musical life was between the years 1854 and 1860, and it was during that time that he attained his wide reputation. In all, one hundred and fifty pieces bear his name as author, and of these a half score or more, at least, are as popular to-day as they ever were, and are known in wider circles, and bid fair to achieve musical immortality.

Foster never sang in public, and never had ambition for distinction in that line. When he sang his own pieces in private, however, he rendered them with a depth of feeling that commanded rapt attention, and evoked the responsive sympathies of his hearers. His voice was a baritone, pleasing, but weak. He was fond of family singing, and some of his songs were written for use in the circle of friends and kindred who frequented the old home in Pittsburgh.

In 1850 Foster was married to Miss Jane McDowell, the daughter of Dr. A. N. McDowell, a leading physician of Pittsburgh. Shortly after this he removed to New York, but after a short residence in that city returned to Pittsburgh. In 1860 he once more took up his residence in New York, where he remained until his death.

THE UNTIMELY END OF LIFE.

While staying at the American Hotel, in New York, he was attacked with fever and ague, but seemed to be in no serious danger. On the 12th of January, while engaged in dressing, he fainted and fell, but recovered consciousness thereafter, and on the following day peacefully fell asleep. He died on the 13th of January, 1864, before he had reached his thirty-eighth year. His remains were taken to his beloved Pittsburgh for interment. On the 21st of January the funeral services were held in Trinity Church and were conducted by Rev. E. C. Swope, then the rector.

The church was crowded to its utmost capacity with his mourning fellow citizens, who took a just pride in his genius and national reputation. He was buried in the old Allegheny Cemetery, not far from the spot where he was born. As the remains passed through the gate a group of musicians sang, "Come Where My Love Lies Dreaming." When the brief burial service was ended and the coffin was lowered into the grave the musicians present joined with those at the tomb to sing the strains of that immortal melody, "Old Folks at Home."

There Stephen C. Foster lies beside the mother that he so loved in life. A simple gravestone marks the place where he sleeps. As yet no monument has ever been reared to his memory in his native city or elsewhere. It is a duty which remains to be done and which ought to be done without more than needful delay. The Scotch-Irish Society of Pennsylvania sends forth a voice this night to our brethren of West

Pennsylvania, where so many hardy scions of the race have their homes, invoking them to see to it that this noble son of our Scotch-Irish ancestors, this sweet American singer, shall soon have in some suitable place a fitting monument as a memorial of his services to humanity and the honor which he has conferred upon his beloved native city.

He has sweetened a multitude of lives; he has set in play influences that have brightened homes and hearts beyond number. His songs are ringing still wherever the English tongue is spoken. It is highly becoming that those whom he served so well should give expression to their gratitude by keeping his memory green forever.

The last negro melody which he wrote was "Old Black Joe," which appeared in 1861. This is one of the most beautiful and pathetic of his pieces, and stirs the heart with strong yearning for that blissful immortality upon which we may hope that the singer has entered. It happened to our Scotch-Irish bard somewhat as with the fabled outgiving of the dying swan, " whose sweetest song is the last she sings."

One item upon our menu requires a word of explanation. We have to introduce to you for the first time " Scotch-Irish Pioneer Porridge." You know it well, though not by that name. American Scotch-Irishmen of the old-time sort were brought up, in a large degree, upon mush and milk. Your Council has resolved to present it to you formally and ask you to acknowledge and adopt it as a national dish. What right have we to assume mush and milk—pioneer porridge—to be a typical Scotch-Irish dish? Just as much as New England has to lay a claim to " baked beans and brown bread ! " (Laughter and applause.) We propose to have priority in this matter. If I may use a scientific phrase, we will pre-empt " Mush and Milk " as a Scotch-Irish pioneer dish. Mush and Milk forever ! All hail, Pioneer Porridge ! Gentlemen, rise and receive your racial dish with all the honors !

A procession of waiters here entered the banquet room bearing large bowls of mush and milk with wooden spoons. The musicians struck up a lively Irish tune, and amid much merriment and applause the guests unanimously adopted " Pioneer Porridge " as the typical dish of our American ancestors of Scotch-Irish descent.

Now, gentlemen, as our old fathers used to say, " Fall to." I think while we are eating the mush and milk we might have a song. We will have the first and last verses of " Nelly Bly."

The Apollo Quartette here sang " Nelly Bly," and also "Annie Laurie."

Col. A. K. McClure then spoke as follows:—

Mr. President, Members, and Guests of the Pennsylvania Scotch-Irish Society:—Jostling along in the battle of life, with men falling around us upon every side from day to day, it is only now and then that we are called to take pause and remember that death brings to us at times blows from which we never shall entirely recover.

I rise to-night to announce to this Society that on the 14th of September last Charles Watson McKeehan, who has been Secretary and Treasurer of the organization from its beginning, passed away to join the great majority. There is not a member of this Society who could not rise and testify to the beneficent qualities of the man as he was known in his every-day life, as he was known in his profession, as he was known in all public affairs, in which he was ever public spirited, as one whose character stood without blemish before the world. All these things could be told by every member of this Society who has met him at this table from year to year since the Society was first organized.

But I speak of one of whom the word " friendship " has more than common meaning. Those in younger life attach little importance to it, for friends are made every day, and friendships are formed often speedily and as speedily forgotten. When you shall have reached near to the patriarchal age and given half a century of active life in association with men, the word "friendship" has a meaning that others know not of. As friends have become feeble and fallen by the wayside, leaving pangs in the heart and sad memories of love, there is to all this one blessing, that among God's men are those whose friendship becomes brighter and brighter with each returning year, and who become nobler as you get closer to them and see them as they are.

I rise, not to speak of our fallen brother as all would speak of him, who knew him simply as a man of affairs and a man who honored citizenship and manhood. I speak of one whom I knew from boyhood; whom I knew in early life; whom I saw ripen in intelligence, influence, and power; and in whose career, that I have watched from day to day for forty years, I have never seen other than the highest standard of manhood and the grandest devotion to everything that made up the noblest character. And more than that, I can speak of him as others cannot. I saw his filial devotion when sorrow came to his household. It has been so for half his life. I saw the most beautiful attributes of that devotion every year, and I saw him where only you can learn the true value of a man; where you can only learn the highest and noblest and holiest attainments of human character; that is, at the altar of his own home, where purity and affection had their resting place in love and peace.

This is the highest tribute that can be paid to men after all. Without it the character is imperfect. Men may be great, and even achieve greatness; may write their names high up on the scale of fame; but the man whose life is not lovely at the altar of his home is a reproach to himself and his God. I desire to speak of him, of the things which may not be known to all, that his character may be not only understood as grand and noble, as all the world and all his associates viewed it, but as a life that was literally without a blemish, and a life that must live in sweet memories among his associates during their lifetime, like the soft strains of music in evening time upon distant waters.

I ask, Mr. President, that this Society shall make a minute of his death; and I present it that the Secretary may read it,

and that it shall be placed upon the records of this Society.
(Applause.)

The President :—

The Secretary will read the minute presented by Colonel
McClure.

Mr. Fisher (reading) :—

CHARLES WATSON McKEEHAN.

Charles Watson McKeehan, Secretary and Treasurer of this
Society since its organization, passed away from earthly sor-
rows on the 14th of September, 1895. He was one of the
most active of the men who organized the Scotch-Irish Society of Pennsylvania, and has been its most laborious official
from its first meeting until his death. While well known and
respected in the community in which he lived, there was no
circle that so well understood and so highly appreciated him
as this little assembly that now gives expression to its sorrow
over the bereavement that has befallen it. He was a typical
Scotch-Irishman; resolutely honest, broad, and progressive in
intelligence, faithful in every duty to the public, to himself, and
to home, and performed to the best of his ability every responsibility that was placed upon him. He stood high at the
bar, alike in character and attainments, and was foremost
among the best of citizens, public spirited in everything that
pertained to the public welfare, and thoroughly conscientious
in all things. Above all, he illustrated the noblest attributes
of mankind in his friendships and in the holier duties of home
and household. Wherever he was best known he was most
beloved, and his memory will linger as sweet incense with all
who knew him until their latest day. The loss of such a man
is a loss to the community, a loss to the State, a loss to civilization, and there is eminent fitness in this expression of our
sorrow for one so efficient and beloved, who fell in the race
when in full mental and physical vigor, with every prospect of
long-continued usefulness. To those who mourn him in his
desolated home we send sincerest sympathy for their bereavement of one whose loss is keenly felt by all of his brethren in

this circle, and to all we can commend his high example as worthy of emulation.

The President :—

Gentlemen, you have heard this minute and the motion that it be spread upon our records. Is it your pleasure that it shall be adopted? If so will you signify it by a rising vote? (All rising.) It is so ordered.

After dinner the President spoke as follows :—

I do not want to interrupt the gastronomic and social exercises before me any more than is necessary. But the time has come when the speaking of the evening should begin; and I feel called upon, before introducing the first speaker, whom you will, I am sure, listen to with a great deal of cordiality, to explain the somewhat startling discrepancy between the promise of our programme and its fulfillment.

No guest this evening can feel more keenly the disappointment than your officers felt when we found this morning that all but one of our speakers had sent excuses. We were in a profoundly crushed condition. I have a ministerial friend, Dr. Poor, who for a long time was the Secretary of our Presbyterian Board of Ministerial Relief, who is an incorrigible wit. He enjoys a good joke even at his own expense, like a true wit. He was once traveling to New York, a commercial suburb of manufacturing Philadelphia of which you have heard. It was a warm day, and he put his silk hat in the vacant seat in front of him, and was soon lost in the contents of the morning paper. Presently along came a gentleman, the doctor busy with his paper, and edged his way into the vacant seat. Quite unobservant of the silent silken occupant he slowly sank down. There was a sharp explosion of crackling sounds. The stranger had sat upon the doctor's hat. He rose in consternation, and, seizing the wrinkled remnants of the tile, turn to the doctor and exclaimed, "Sir, sir, I—I—I beg pardon! Is this your silk hat?" "Well," says the doctor, drawling forth the words, and casting a droll look upon the flattened object, "it *was* my silk hat, but now it is—sat in (satin)." (Laughter.) That was our condition this morning. We felt very much sat in, and sat upon. But we did the best we could under such short notice to get good substitutes for the absentees. We were gladdened to find that at the last hour Colonel Cassells had come in from Washington, bringing one trophy with him—"the noblest Roman of them all." (Applause.) We can say that truthfully and also safely—inasmuch as the other fellows are not here.

Now, I think I ought to say with regard to the absent gentlemen that, with one exception, there were positive promises that they would speak for us this evening. It is due to your Council to say this much. It is due to our absent friends to state their reasons for absence. Senator Burroughs is lying sick with the grippe. We wish him a speedy deliverance from the same. Death in Mr. Allen's family compelled him to leave Washington, and, of course, he could not come here. He has our cordial sympathy in his bereavement. The other gentlemen are staying away on account of the pending "Bond Bill," upon which a vote is likely to be taken to-night. They are, like St. Paul of old, "ambassadors in bonds" (laughter), and their liberty is therefore abridged. Your Council was naturally inclined to think their absence a needless devotion to their country's interests, when "pairs" can so easily be obtained. But we cannot in good conscience censure conscientious representatives for doing what they feel to be their duty. The only other gentleman not "present or accounted for" is Bishop Thompson, and it is proper to say concerning him that we only had a conditional promise from him.

One of the gentlemen who was to speak has redeemed his promise. He is the only "representative" from Washington, and he is a Senator. (Laughter.) We may hope that he comes with all the bottled eloquence of all the gentlemen who would or should have been here. I will waste none of your time in introducing him. He has a great many titles. He was a Captain during the "late unpleasantness" with our Southern fellow citizens. I was down in that direction myself about that time, Senator (addressing Senator Lindsay), and we were all glad enough to get away. He has been a Judge, a Member of the House of Representatives, and he is now the successor in the Senate of Mr. Carlisle, who is known, perhaps, to some of you who are interested in the current bond sales. I have only this to say in high commendation of the qualifications of this gentleman who is to speak to us, that he has just told me privately that he takes our pioneer porridge, "mush and milk," every morning for breakfast. (Applause.) I do not wonder that, under such a Scotch-Irish diet, he has developed to such proportions, physically, intellectually, and politically. He is of the "blood royal," there is no doubt of that, and he comes from Kentucky, that dark and bloody ground, the home land of many great and gallant Scotch-Irishmen, and of fair and noble women without number. I have the honor and pleasure to introduce to you Senator Lindsay, of Kentucky. (Applause.)

Senator Lindsay :—

MR. PRESIDENT AND GENTLEMEN:—By way of allaying apprehensions which may be very reasonably entertained, I wish to say at the outset that I am not the Senator who, on one occasion, spoke fifteen hours without cessation ; nor am I the Senator who took eight days to tell the people how much he knew about silver coinage.

I speak here to-night, under great embarrassment, to an audience made up of citizens of a State which has three avowed candidates for the Presidency. I feel that I am not only in the land of greatness, but of Presidential possibilities.

I had the honor and pleasure, several years since, to attend a Scotch-Irish Congress, held in the city of Louisville, and I observed one peculiarity about that particular Congress, and that was, that during the four or five days of almost uninterrupted speaking, every man who spoke spoke well of himself and all his kindred (laughter and applause), and I suppose that it will be in order for me now and here to follow that most excellent sample.

I feel, here in Pennsylvania, that I am in the very seed-bed of the American Scotch-Irish. Tradition tells me that my ancestry first found the United States somewhere in this vicinity ; that they looked around upon the rich lands of Pennsylvania, and then turned their eyes southward, between the Blue Ridge and the Allegheny, and made their homes in Virginia, in a land which flows with milk and honey. They looked across the Allegheny Mountains, and they heard the stories of what might be found in Kentucky, and immediately took up the line of march for the rich country in which they helped to lay the foundation for a future Commonwealth.

There are many reasons why we should be proud of our race. It was the progenitor of true Americanism. The early colonists clung to the Atlantic Coast, and looked longingly back to the flesh pots across the great water. Our Puritan people, who, like the Scotch-Irish, are inclined to speak well of themselves, remained truly British until the bad laws of the British Government converted them into American rebels. The Cavaliers (we call them Cavaliers because it seems to please them), who settled about the mouth of the James, never forgot to send their children home to England to be educated, until at last Patrick Henry, a Scotch-Irishman, pointed the road to liberty. (Applause.) But it was not so with the Scotch-Irish. After they had finished administering upon the estates of the Irishmen who owned Ulster, they took their way across the Atlantic ; and if a Scotch-Irishman ever looked back I have never heard of it. They did not stay by the Atlantic ; they took their line of march southward and westward. They settled the western valleys of Pennsylvania ; they settled the valleys of Virginia ; they poured over the mountains into western North Carolina ; before the first gun of the Revolution had been fired they were finding their way across the Alleghenies into Kentucky ; and on the day the first gun of the Revolution was fired a party of Scotch-Irishmen, in the middle of what is now the blue grass country, formed a settlement, and when the news came across the mountain that this gun, which sounded around the world, had been fired, they named that place Lexington in honor thereof, and it is called Lexington to-day. While Washington and the Pennsylvanians and the Virginians and the New Englanders were struggling against the British Army along the coast, away off in Kentucky, five hundred miles from the borders of civilization, a Scotch-Irishman, George Rogers Clark, at the Falls of the Ohio, organized an expedition of less than one hundred and fifty men, took his way across the pathless wilderness, captured Kaskaskia and Vincennes, and held all the great Northwest; and it may be said that except for his success the Northwest might have remained a British possession. We held the Southwest by a thread that threatened to break at any time, but the Scotch-Irishman, Andrew Jackson, went down to that country and settled our title forever. (Applause.)

Sam Houston, another Scotch-Irishman (applause)—(I had the honor to be born within three miles of the spot where Sam Houston first saw the light)—Sam Houston, leading a band of Scotch-Irishmen, liberated Texas. Everywhere we find that Scotch-Irish enterprise, Scotch-Irish pluck, and Scotch-Irish prowess have made their mark. Lewis and Clark, who found the way up the Missouri and across the Rocky Mountains, were Scotch-Irishmen whose ancestors had fought in the Revolutionary war.

This much I feel I have a right to say, and am bound to say, in order to keep in the line of the Scotch-Irish oratory of these modern days.

Kentucky was a Scotch-Irish settlement. The Logans, the Todds, the Prestons, and the McClungs—all good Scotch-Irish names—led the way to that country. They took up all the good land they could find. (Laughter.) Nobody else was able to settle the question of the Indians' title, but they settled it by the good old Scotch-Irish plan. They found lands richer than their ancestors had found in Ulster, and their descendants hold them to this day.

Kentucky very early commenced enforcing the Monroe doctrine. As soon as the Scotch-Irish got a foothold there they declared that no part of Kentucky was longer open to colonization. You can come in if you come our way. And Kentucky has been following in that line ever since.

There was one break amongst the Scotch-Irish about thirty-five years ago, and it was a bad break. Scotch-Irish from Pennsylvania went down to see their Scotch-Irish friends on the other side of the Potomac. They got receptions such as possibly they had not anticipated—at Fredericksburg, Chancellorsville, and at other places. But it was Stonewall Jackson's way; we could not help it. Time, at last, set all things even, and the Pennsylvania Scotch-Irish stayed with us until they were content to return home of their own accord; and here we are all together, still praising ourselves and still laying hands upon everything we can take without violating the law. (Laughter.)

I did not come for the purpose of taking up the time that ought to have been appropriated to the gentlemen who agreed to come and did not. I am satisfied, except for my coming, as a scalp hanging to the belt of my friend Cassels, he would not have been here. He showed a great deal of trepidation as we approached Philadelphia, and I could feel his heart beat as he came up the stairs in anticipation of a reception that might not have been such as he desired. But he is here, safe amongst hospitable people.

The President:—

He deserves a cheer.

Senator Lindsay (continuing) :—

I wish to say in behalf of those gentlemen who did not come, and had no better excuse than that they remained in Washington from a sense of duty, that, in my opinion, not one of them is a Scotch-Irishman ; there is not one of them who is a Scotchman or an Irishman either. In my opinion, they are all descended from the "blasted Britishers," and are in sympathy with those people across the water who want to extend their boundaries in Venezuela in defiance of our American idea of the Monroe doctrine. I have listened to several Scotch-Irish speeches on that question, and every one of them breathed out threats of coming slaughter unless Queen Victoria and Salisbury should take the back track. I have no doubt those speeches reached the other side. I have been much pleased in reading what Harcourt, Balfour, and others have had to say to find them moderate, conservative, good natured, and good tempered. They give every assurance that we shall not have to fight over Venezuela. I attribute all this to the bold way in which the Scotch-Irishmen have spoken upon the floor of Congress. Cleveland is a Scotch-Irishman, and Davis, who reported the resolutions which have not yet been voted upon, but which will settle our right to manage everybody's business on the face of the earth, is a Scotch-Irishman of the most undoubted type. Senator Lodge and others from New England were doing a good deal of talking, but when Davis got hold of the matter he put it beyond the region of talk. (Laughter.)

I wish to express my gratification at having the opportunity to meet this distinguished assemblage and to say that I have been more than repaid for my trip over from Washington. I shall bear in mind this evening so long as I live, and when I return to old Kentucky, where the sun still shines, notwithstanding some political complications we have on hand (laughter), I shall not fail to tell the people out there that Philadelphia, or at least the Scotch-Irish of Philadelphia, are good people to meet with and to be with. (Applause.)

Singing by the Apollo Quartette, "My Old Kentucky. Home."

The President :—

Most of us date our claim to be members of this Society one, two, three, or even four generations from the present. But we have a gentleman with us to-night who has the honor—surely Scotch-Irishmen must think it an honor—of claiming by birthright upon the old sod membership in this Society. You will be glad to hear from him. He is one of the foremost of our Philadelphia divines and one of the most learned of those who have come to contribute to the best elements of American and Philadelphia life. He bears a name which has already been referred to in your hearing, and which is just now upon all tongues—Munro. Whether or no he is of the same kin or clan with the original author of the "Monroe doctrine," he is certainly Dr. Munro, and he will speak for himself. (Applause.)

Rev. Dr. J. H. Munro :—

Mr. CHAIRMAN :—I was brought up in the North of Ireland, where we were taught that good doctrine was the foundation of a good life and heroic character, and therefore I very naturally adopt the Monroe doctrine on this side of the water, believing that it is a doctrine which ought to be upheld in all its integrity. I regret very much that the other distinguished gentlemen who were to come from Washington did not appear with Senator Lindsay. After his delightful speech I have no doubt we should have been roused by still further eloquence. I regret it all the more because I am now standing here taking some of the time that the distinguished visitors would have occupied. Perhaps you will regret it still more when I have done, or, perhaps, before I have done.

We are very much, to-night, in the position of a priest who went into a Dublin restaurant a year or two ago on a fast day. "Waiter," he said, "bring me some fish." "I am sorry to tell your reverence all the fish are gone. It is a fast day, and there is a great demand." "Well," said he, "you will have to do the best you can, then ; bring me some beefsteak ; the Lord knows I asked for fish." (Laughter.) Our Chairman has done the very best to bring you royal fish from Washington, and he has landed one, but in the present case I fear you will have to be content with some beefsteak, perhaps a little tough and a little dry.

The brethren who were born on this side can tell you of the deeds of the Scotch-Irish in this country. Will you pardon me if I tell you one or two things about the state of affairs in the old home ?

I visited Ireland two or three years ago, and was delighted to find that its prosperity, especially in the North, was just about as great as its hospitality. If any of you go there you will be almost killed with kindness. You will have to eat your way through about six meals every day, and drink prodigious quantities of tea, and very strong tea.

Throughout the North the country has improved very much within the last twenty or twenty-five years. You will not see finer farming in any part of the world, not even in the famous lowlands of Scotland. The farm houses are much better than they were, and even the houses on small farms are now having wooden floors and carpets, where formerly they had only clay floors, stamped upon with the feet to make them hard enough. In the houses you will find evidences of comfort and of taste, all showing that the prosperity of the people is increasing. There is more money in the savings banks to-day in Ireland than there has ever been in the history of the past. One reason of this increased prosperity is found in the land laws which have been passed within the last twenty to twenty-five years, beginning with the great Act carried through Parliament by Mr. Gladstone. I think that the folk on this side of the water are not aware that Ireland at the present time has probably the best land laws of any country upon the face of the earth. That improvement was needed. They secured a law which was known by the name of " The Three F's "— fixity of tenure, free sale, fair rent. Now those three F's covered the great grievance that was known as the land question. First, fixity of tenure. About three-fourths of the farmers, up to the time this legislation was passed, could be dispossessed at the mere will of the landlord. These laws now give the farmer permanent tenure of his land, so that he can only be dispossessed either for non-payment of rent or for a destructive use of the farm. The second F was free sale. Under the former system the farmer could not sell to the highest bidder; he must sell to the person chosen by the landlord, and at a price fixed by the landlord. When my father sold a large farm that he possessed he was compelled to take £1000 less than he could have obtained. The law now allows a man to sell to a buyer of good character, and at the largest price he is able to obtain. Still more important is fair rent. In the old time, and in mine, many of the landlords raised the rent to the very highest sum that the land would bear. The worst landlords were not the old nobles, but were the merchants who had become rich and who had bought the land merely as a speculation. If a farmer turned a piece of bog into a field he was charged high rent for his own improvements. Fair rent was one of the demands of that date. And how was this secured? A land court was created, composed of an attorney and two experts in land. Either the landlord or the tenant could appear before that court—the landlord if he thought the rent was too low; the tenant if he thought the rent was too high. The court heard evidence; they examined the farm; they took into account the average prices of produce for the last five or ten years; they fixed a rent, and that judicial rent, as it was called, was binding upon the tenant and the landlord for a fixed term of years. The result was that throughout the whole of Ireland the rents were reduced about a third, and in consequence the tenants have been prospering ever since.

And there is still another piece of legislation that was secured and is still being encouraged by both the great political parties. A bill was passed by which the tenants could buy their farms outright from landlords who were willing to sell. The value of these farms was usually from fifteen to twenty times the amount of the annual rent. The government advanced, if not the whole, at least three-fourths of the purchase money, at five per cent. interest. By paying interest for thirty-nine years the mortgage was declared paid off, and the farm becomes the property of the tenant. The government was able to carry through this financial transaction, because, Senator, they borrowed at two and a half per cent. over there, whatever the reason is, and used the other two and a half per cent. as a sinking fund in favor of the tenant, so that at the end of thirty-nine years the tenant enjoys the farm as his own and absolute property. And hundreds of tenants in the North of Ireland have availed themselves of this beneficent law. I question whether one item of that law could be passed in this country, because it would be pronounced unconstitutional. And therefore, gentlemen, I say that at the present time there is practically no land question in Ireland, and the few irritating things that remain will very soon be settled. The English and Scotch farmers are complaining that Ireland is favored at the expense of the United Kingdom. So the land question that has been the great trouble in Ireland is now practically settled; and if you will go to the North of Ireland and the South, I will venture to say that you will see the country smiling and blossoming like the rose.

There is just one other thing I should like to say, and it was suggested by Dr. Patton and Judge Ferguson, who, I suppose, ran away lest they should be called upon to make speeches. When I was young we were all brought up to attend churches with great regularity. Those churches, of course, were very plain buildings; but if you went now to Ireland you would find that the churches are becoming very beautiful. You know they had great prejudices against singing anything like paraphrases and hymns, and it was a sin to sing anything but psalms. Not only that, but there were only twelve or fifteen "inspired tunes" which were proper to be sung in the presence of God. I may say, lest I forget it, that now both hymns and organs are tolerated in the Irish Presbyterian Church, although they are not sanctioned by authority. The Rev. Dr. Cook, who was one of the great champions of orthodoxy, actually cut the paraphrases and hymns out of his psalm book. The Rev. Dr. McNaughton went to a country church to preach a collection sermon (they are great there on collection sermons), and he unfortunately gave out a paraphrase—"Let us praise God by singing" such and such a paraphrase. The precentor was sitting below the box pulpit, like an egg cup, in which the ministers there preach, and he turned around and said: "Sir, we don't sing paraphrases here." "Very well, sir; let us sing to the praise of God the second version of the one hundred and thirty-sixth psalm." "We cannot sing that psalm here." "Well, since you won't sing paraphrases and can't sing psalms, let us pray."

Senator Lindsay has mentioned that in certain regions of Kentucky there is something stronger to be had than milk and honey. I think the Senator said that. I believe the same is true in the North of Ireland. On market days some very worthy Presbyterians, even elders, would take a drop too much. Such conduct there, even now, is not considered a very heinous sin. We must make allowance for it as due to social customs. There was a very worthy man of this kind who sat three or four pews before my father's pew. The Rev. Dr. Johnson was preaching to our congregation that day, and at the close of the service he gave out the beautiful paraphrase:—

"O God of Bethel, by whose hand
Thy people still are fed;
Who, through this weary wilderness,
Hath all our fathers led."

Up rose this man, " Sir, Mr. Johnson, we don't sing paraphrases here." " My good man, you might do something worse. We will sing the sixty-seventh psalm, ' Lord, bless and pity us.' " And of course the congregation sang that in the most delightful style imaginable.

Senator Lindsay has well said that the Scotch-Irish had a part, and not the least honorable part, in founding this great Republic, and in fighting the battles of liberty. Gentlemen, many of their greatest battles were not fought in this country, but were fought upon the old sod. There, in times of persecution, our fathers remained true to their consciences and true to their God. Men were chained and lay rotting in prison for years on account of their religion ; tender women were driven to the woods to escape the unchaste violence of their persecutors, but they stood firm, some remaining in the old home and others coming to this country, where they have acted as you have heard Senator Lindsay describe to-night.

I think that this is one of the greatest illustrations of the Word of our Lord, that they who suffer persecutions for His sake shall receive manifold more in this life. On account of what those old fathers suffered in Ireland we enjoy the manifold more in this country of freedom and unbounded prosperity. It was Scotch-Irish courage in the South as well as in the North that won freedom for this country ; and what those old fathers had not, when they left their homes to found this Republic of ours, where the churches are larger than they are in the old country, and where we stand in the very front

van of Christian liberty, we have " manyfold." Now, gentlemen, I have done ; and I think you will feel very much as the
Sunday-school scholars when they were reading of Philip and
the eunuch, and were asked, " Why did the eunuch go on his
way rejoicing ? " " Because Philip had a done preaching."

The President :—

I have heard of a certain statesman who bought a dictionary
and afterward came to the storekeeper to complain about it.
"Sir," he said, " this dictionary is defective." " Why, no ; it
is not." " Yes, it is ! " " What is the matter ? " " Sir, I
have looked all through the f's and I can't find ' fysician '
(physician)." We are glad to learn from our friend, Dr.
Munro, and his report from the old sod that you *can* find the
true " physician " for Ireland and under the f's—three of
them ? And we will remember these three " F's " which he
has brought to us. I think, too, that his allusion to the battles
of the old country must have struck a sympathetic chord in the
minds of our singers. Possibly it is a case of telephony, but
I fancied that I heard the strain of " Boyne Water " gently
breathing from the quarter where they sit, and if they can now
give us a verse of that immortal, unmusical, and battle-provok-
ing ballad, then they may sing after that No. 11 of our selections, " I'm off to Philadelphia in the Mornin'." Stephen
Foster did not write that song, but it is a good one and a very
popular one in England.

" Boyne Water " was then sung by a member of
the Apollo Quartette amid much applause and laughter, after which the quartette sang " Off to Philadelphia in the Mornin'."

The President :—

Our Scotch-Irish ancestors had a proverb, " Comb seldom,
comb sore ! " That is why we feel that on such occasions as
these, when we get " into a corner," as it were, we may
call on certain individuals more frequently than on others.
They are so used to the " combing " that they do not get sore

under it. We have present one who, to quote another proverb, is "like cold souse, always ready." (Laughter.) He is quite able to take the absent bishop's place, although not himself a bishop—except *in futuro*. (Applause.) We know he will make a good bishop because he is a good Scotch-Irishman, whose ancestral ministers are all "bishops." In fact, I do not know what would have become of the Protestant churches of this country if it had not been for the Scotch-Irish who have enriched all denominations by the contributions of vigorous material, both clerical and lay. I have great pleasure in introducing to you our friend and ex-President, Dr. McConnell. (Applause.)

Dr. McConnell :—

MR. CHAIRMAN AND GENTLEMEN:—The despotic habit of our presiding officer reminds me of a story that is told of a Scotch girl, who was an applicant before the Session, and was asked to recite the question in the catechism, "What are the decrees of God?" "Na, na," she replied, "He kens that best Himsel'." There is nobody kens the decrees of this Society as well as the President himself. (Laughter.)

Being asked at a moment's warning to say a word concerning the Scotch-Irish, it is indeed difficult to know what to say. It has been said here, or something like it, a moment ago that the Scotch-Irish in this country have been, in a certain degree, characteristically deficient in the arts and the belles-lettres. I think that the President was, perhaps, not well advised when he even intimated that the Scotch-Irish in America were lacking in poetry. Why only a few moments ago, without an instant's warning, an ex-President of this Society dashed off with his running pencil, without even taking time to think, such a verse as this :—

> " Whether the dog was faithful
>   Is certainly doubtful to say ;
> For how could a dog that is faithful
>   Be truthfully said to be Tray (betray)?"

for which our friend, ex-President Porter, is responsible.

It is exceedingly difficult to say anything about the Scotch-Irish in America, because it is but another way of being called upon to speak for America itself. We are at a very serious disadvantage, our Scotch-Irish Society in Philadelphia and elsewhere, as compared, for example, with the New England Society. When there are but a few people, and when they are marked off from the great mass of the population, there is always a tendency in them to draw together, and there is some excuse for them to magnify their ancestry, their works, and their future. I think this is the reason why the New England Society and the New England Society's dinner in this and other great cities is always such a marked occasion. It is because there are so few of them. (Laughter.) Now, when it comes to speak of the Scotch-Irish, it is practically being called upon to speak for the whole United States, because, if you really come to consider it, the one ingredient which has entered into and constituted this magnificent blend which we call the American character, the one ingredient which dominates all others, is the Scotch-Irish. That is simply a matter of history. They began to make themselves felt at the mouth of the Kennebec, and their influence slowly ascended the great river; it crept away around to the north of the New Englanders, and unconsciously dominated even the Puritan. It made itself felt at the mouth of the Hudson, and from there traveled west across the great interior of the Empire State, and mixed itself with that stream of New Englandism which has propagated itself across the whole northern frontier of the United States. It planted itself at the mouth of the James and it spread over into Kentucky, and we have seen what it has done there in the production of Senator Lindsay. (Laughter and applause.) It planted itself on the coast of North Carolina and produced the first Declaration of Independence. It crossed over into valleys and troughs of the Allegheny Valley range, and it really dominated New Orleans. The truth is, the Scotch-Irish has dominated the whole United States, so that it has become difficult for us here or elsewhere to organize and maintain a Scotch-Irish Society; that is really the secret of whatever difficulty there may be in the maintenance of an organization of this kind. There are too many of us. Our inheritance is shared by so many that that which is really so valuable, and which we are intelligent enough to refer to its real source, is simply the Americanism which has spread all over this country.

Now I, for one, am devoutly thankful for this. When they came here they were all Presbyterians and Calvinists. The wisest of them have got over that. (Laughter.) The people of this country have drifted away from that, but they have not moved from under its influence. They have carried with them all over the country certain characteristics which belong to that peculiar people for which three continents were sifted in order that it might be planted in this soil. The result of that sifting was not the New Englander, but was the Scotch-Irishman.

I cannot help but think, from reading the newspapers lately, and from looking at the movement of society, that maybe the thing which we speak of so little and treat with a jest, the characteristic quality of Scotch-Irishmen, which has come to be the characteristic quality of Americans, may be a quality which will be drawn upon more largely in the near future than ever before in the history of the United States or in the history of the world. As we are drawing to the close of the century which has included in it more changes, which has created more history than all the antecedent history of the world put together, there seems to be a sort of a feeling universally prevalent that we are standing at the gateway of marvelous things. I think we are. I do not think that any one can look over the situation of the world at this moment without being tempted to lay aside for a little his light and jesting mood, or avoid being compelled to think soberly of what may confront us in not only the generation that comes after this, but possibly in the generation of which we form a part.

There are great questions that have gradually been shaping themselves and are coming before the world for settlement. There are questions of government, of administration, of justice ; questions of equity. The Old World has lamentably lately shown itself impotent to settle these great questions.

The fundamental, essential questions of principle, of right, and fair, and honorable, and just dealing between man and man will not be settled in England, nor in Germany, nor in Russia, nor in France. They will be settled in the United States. The people of this country have lately, in the Venezuela affair, it seems to me, shown a disposition to settle the fundamental questions of human society in a way which no other nation has shown itself ready to do. I believe in all sincerity that the disposition to settle questions upon right and equitable, conscientious and God-fearing principles is due, more than to any other one source, to those habits of thought and action which our God-fearing and thoughtful and canny ancestors imported to these shores.

I do not think we truly realize what the history of these United States of ours imports. There have been in the history of this Republic three great wars. During the same period there have been fifty wars on the other side of the water. On the other side of the water every conflict has revolved about some question either of self or national interest. In the United States every war that we have fought has revolved about a question of principle. The difference is radical. In the Old World every conflict has revolved about a question of advantage, the gaining of territory, the securing of indemnity, the securing of some political advantage. In this country every war that we have been engaged in has revolved about some question of abstract principle. It is true with regard to our original War of Independence ; it was true with regard to our War of 1812 ; it was pre-eminently true with regard to our great Civil War. It was a war of abstract principle ; and this could not be carried on in any nation whose antecedents had not been deeply grounded in that habit of thinking upon the principles of things and fighting for them.

Now, I cannot help thinking that we, in these United States, the people that we sometimes criticise, whose government we sometimes criticise, and possibly with justice, have a record which no other nation has. We have done things in this country that no other people in the history of God's earth have ever done. We have, with all our faults and defects, kept more closely to what we believe to be the wish and law of Almighty God than any other people have ever kept.

A very distinguished citizen of Philadelphia called attention, in my hearing, not long ago, to the fact that in the only war for conquest, the only fight for aggrandizement, that this country has ever been engaged in, a very peculiar thing happened. Nearly fifty years ago these people (who are all Scotch-Irish) fought a war for conquest. The result of that war was the acquisition of an enormous extent of valuable territory—Texas, and the land lying westward and northward of it. We won it, it is true, at the mouth of the cannon, but having done so we did what no nation under heaven has ever done— we not only did not lay any indemnity upon the conquered foe, but we deliberately paid the conquered for the ground which we had taken. No other nation has ever done anything of the sort. Lately this country of ours has been challenged— some have said rudely, and some have said inadvisedly; I do not believe either of these accusations—they have been challenged to give their opinion upon the question of how the whole civilized world should be required to treat all questions of territory upon the American continent. Their answer was precisely in keeping with the quality and character that the people of these United States have inherited. The President has announced to the world, and in my judgment has announced rightly, and also in my judgment has timely made the announcement, that upon this American continent every question of territory shall be settled, not by force, but by legal right. I do not think that anything has occurred in the history of this country which ought to give a thoughtful man more hope for the moral soundness of the community than the way in which the people of these United States have responded to the challenge of the Chief Executive in the matter of the extension of British territory in Venezuela.

Now notice exactly what has occurred. I am not an advocate for the Chief Executive of this country, or for any other Chief Executive, but I wish to call your attention to this: The claim has been made that for this whole American continent the principle upon which questions of territory and extension

of empire are finally determined in the Old World shall not
obtain. In the Old World it is solved purely by force. " Let
him take who has the power; let him keep who can." We
have said that in this country he shall not take who can; he
shall take only after the serious, sober deliberate judgment of
the civilized world upon the equities of the case. The Chief
Executive has said so. Both branches of the legislative department have immediately given their universal indorsement to
that ; and the people of the United States, being taken off their
guard, at once gave their unanimous consent to what is but the
traditional way of looking at things—which we have inherited
from our Scotch-Irish ancestors—that these questions shall be
settled with the view to the intrinsic right of things, and not
with sole reference to the power of the stronger. This does
not involve any question of party politics. It simply seems to
me to be the last and the most striking of the manifestations of
that spirit in which, in the Scotch-Irish, takes a theological
form, in some places a doctrinal form, but all over the United
States takes a profoundly and unconsciously ethical form. We
all believe in God ; we believe in right ; we believe in justice;
we believe in it so much that we are willing to go out of our
way to insist that justice shall be done. Now this quality in
the United States is the same quality which insisted upon singing psalms and not paraphrases; which originally insisted
upon being Calvinistic, but which has now grown broader,
more liberal, more generous, and is willing to allow a wider
difference of opinion among the children of the same ancestry,
but which still insists that all the children of the same ancestry
shall be faithful to what they believe to be the behests of
Almighty God. (Applause.)

The President :—

We had with us a little while ago the President of that
peculiar Philadelphia institution, the Clover Club (Colonel
McClure). We have still with us as one of our guests a
gentleman who is ranked as one of the bards of that institution. We will call on him for a song—Mr. Coussans.
Then we will hear from another of our ex-Presidents, alluded

to by our last speaker as having disproved your present President's statement that the power of song writing has vanished from the Scotch-Irish population—Mr. Porter.

Mr. Coussans then sang "The Gypsy Fires are Shining."

The President :—

We will now hear "a word" from Mr. Porter.

Mr. W. W. Porter :—

MR. PRESIDENT AND GENTLEMEN :—I saw in a paper the other day a toast that was new to me. It was, " To the ladies (God bless them) ; once our superiors, now our equals." The new woman is one of the moving questions of the day. Every man wants to keep in touch with the literature which bears upon current matter, so I turned with some interest to peruse recently a cook book. It had numberless recipes in it. One particularly caught my attention. After prescribing with medical accuracy the constituents of the viand to be produced, these instructions followed: "Sit on the stove." This alone, perhaps, might be thought to be irritating, but to this super-fluous instruction was added, " Stir continuously." Ever since I dashed off that "gem of poetry" which Dr. McConnell has read I have felt in the condition of the cook. I have been stirring continuously in fear that I might be called on to speak.

Listening to Dr. Munro, I was much impressed by one fact. I think we all understood that if Irishmen, and especially the tenantry, are anything they are sportsmanlike, but judging by the present condition, as he depicts it, of the landlord law, half of the fun of the tenantry is gone. It was a bad day when a tenant could not go out over there and shoot a landlord or two, and now the sport seems to be over.

I find in this gentleman whom Dr. McCook has eulogized— Stephen Collins Foster—a most prophetic mind. You and I have observed in Philadelphia, as people elsewhere have observed, the passing of the darkey. We look upon our former cobblestone streets, and we remember we saw there the ebony-hued laborer. He has been superseded, and we find there now the swarthy Italian. In these songs of Mr. Foster, a copy of which you have before you, that condition of things was prophesied. I ask you, brethren, to turn to hymn No. 4.

The President :—

Sing if you please.

Mr. Porter (continuing) :—

Look at verse No. 2. You find there the passing of the darkey and the oncoming of the Italian. Listen :—

> "They hunt no more for the 'possum and the coon,
>   On the meadow, the hill, and the shore;
> They sing no more by the glimmer of the moon,
>   On the bench by the old cabin door.
> The day goes (Dagoes) by like a shadow o'er the heart,
>   With sorrow where all was delight;
> The time has come when the darkies have to part,
>   Then, my old Kentucky home, good night."

Thus we find that the genius of the Scotch-Irish contains not only the melody of verse, but prophetic vision. (Laughter.)

Finally, gentlemen, I have always felt, and I think most of us have felt, that this Society had a father. I regret that he has not been able to remain until this stage of our meeting. Colonel McClure, I think, is regarded (being the first President) as the father of this Society. I have been casting about as to what we shall dub our present acting President. He can't be the father, but by looking at the theme of his discourse I find a suggestion which perhaps you will adopt—I pledge you Dr. McCook, our "Foster"-father. (Laughter.)

The President :—

Well, that is Irish wit for you! I have often heard of the men who could find the traditional "nigger in the wood pile," but it is reserved for a Scotch-Irish ex-President to find a "Dago" in a negro minstrel's song. I think I may venture to call on Mr. William Righter Fisher at this point; and afterward, before we have one or two short "spurts" that are to follow, before we go home, I would suggest that we sing Foster's "Oh, Susanna." We have had a good many solemn songs to-night, and this rollicking piece may be an agreeable change. Now we will hear Mr. Fisher's report as Secretary and Treasurer.

Mr. Fisher :—

MR. PRESIDENT AND GENTLEMEN :—I have but very few words to say, and they shall mainly relate to the general condition of our Society. When I came here the Treasurer's report was in my pocket, but I see it has disappeared during my rather free and unsuspecting circulation about these tables. (Laughter.) I assure you it is no great loss to the Society and no possible gain to him who may find it. You will be spared the infliction of its reading. We had, as I recollect, a balance in the treasury of $507 on February 1st of the present year, This is a compact epitome of our financial condition well suited to the hour and to this occasion. It shows what we have to spend, which to most of us is always the item of greatest importance.

The membership of the Society is slightly in excess of two hundred. I had the exact figures on a paper which has disappeared with the report, so I am thrown back upon memory to replace them. In this connection I am reminded of what has been the subject of frequent remark by the members of your Council. It is important and desirable that the membership of this Society be greatly increased, indeed it ought to be doubled. It ought to be more than doubled. The New England Society rallies at its annual banquets in this city a much greater number than the Scotch-Irish have ever gathered about their festive board. It is thought that this should not be the case. The descendants of the Scotch-Irish vastly outnumber the New Englanders in this country, and they have rendered an equal if not a greater service in moulding the life and institutions of the nation, at least in this State, all along the slopes of the Alleghenies, and over the extended regions of the West. It certainly ought to be a matter of honorable pride to us all to have the membership of this Pennsylvania

Society of the Scotch-Irish commensurate with the rôle our ancestors have played in the life of the State. The only way in which such an end can be accomplished is by the members generally scattered over different sections of the State bearing it in mind and sending in nominees for membership. The Council hopes that all who are here will take this to heart, and that the coming year will witness a large increase in the Society's roll.

There is probably one other matter to which I ought to refer, and in doing so let me remind the members that I am only a temporary acting Secretary. I have simply picked up the ends of the work as it was left by our lamented friend, Mr. McKeehan. There is need of a service which the pressure of affairs will not permit me to give. It was suggested here last year that some systematic historic work should be done by the Society. That suggestion was referred back to the Council for their consideration and action, and there has been some little discussion of it. The fruition has been very meagre. The idea is that we ought to form the nucleus of a collection of pamphlets and books bearing on the history of the Scotch-Irish people in this country and abroad, from which the industrious historian may gather data for his work. If this is to be done a beginning must be made, and there is no more effective way of starting the work than for each member of the Society throughout the State to forward to the Secretary any literature of the kind which may fall in his way, and which his Scotch-Irish acquisitiveness will permit him to part with. It will be preserved for the common good.

I hold in my hand a letter from Judge Agnew and another from Dr. MacIntosh, both of whom have long been active and valued members of this Society, and who are too well known at these gatherings to need an introduction from me. They send their greetings, and regret their inability to be with us. I am sure we all share in that regret and heartily send our greetings in return to them.

Before closing there is one other duty I feel impelled to perform. Judge Joseph Allison, who has recently deceased, and who was so highly honored and esteemed in his lifetime as a model member of the judiciary of the State, was one of the original members of the Pennsylvania Scotch-Irish Society. Although I have prepared no form of minute to present at this time in commemoration of our appreciation of his friendship and of his noble devotion to duty and right, I think all will agree that such a minute should be spread upon our records. He certainly honored us in his life, and his service and reputation as a judge in this city have been surpassed by none of his contemporaries.

The President :—

You have heard the motion, and it will be proper, perhaps, to suggest that Mr. Fisher and Mr. Porter be appointed a committee to draft the minute provided for. If that is your pleasure will you please signify it by a rising vote? (All rising.) It is so adopted.

We will suspend the singing of "Oh, Susanna," a moment, if you please, just to hear a word from the Committee who have in charge the local arrangements for the next Scotch-Irish Congress. We have with us a gentleman who, judging from his melodious name, ought to have come somewhere from the neighborhood of Castle Blarney, or from those far-famed "banks of Killarney" where once dwelt "sweet Kate Karney." His name is McAlarney, and I hope he will say a few words about the coming Scotch-Irish Congress which is to be held in Harrisburg.

Mr. M. W. McAlarney :—

When the President, Dr. McCook, requested me to extend an invitation to the Scotch-Irish Society of Pennsylvania to attend the approaching congress of the Scotch-Irish Society of America, I protested that I was not "a glib and fluent talker," nor accustomed to making speeches, and that I thought it was rather unfair that I should extend the invitation, considering that we had upon the floor four or five gentlemen from Harrisburg who were much better fitted to extend an invitation of this character than myself. But he, being a Scotch-Irishman and a Presbyterian too, and thoroughly believing, as he said, in foreordination, he declined to accept my excuses and select some other person. I have but a few words to say.

The Scotch-Irish Congress, when it met at Lexington last Summer, asked the committee from Harrisburg sent there to extend an invitation to it to meet in Harrisburg, " Why do you ask us to come to Harrisburg ? " I told them then, as I tell you now, that Harrisburg and Dauphin County, the upper portion of Lebanon Valley, the Valley of the Juniata, and the Valley of the Cumberland, were the very cradle of the Scotch-Irish people of the United States, or at least the largest cradle ; yet in all the speeches that I have heard about this banqueting board I regret to say that I have heard little reference to anything that has transpired in the heart of Pennsylvania, the central part of our great State, from which nearly all of the Scotch-Irishmen present come. Your first President, Colonel McClure, was born on the Juniata ; our lamented Secretary, Mr. McKeehan, was born in the Cumberland Valley ; and I see before me faces of men in almost every walk of life who represent Scotch-Irish families on the west branch of the Susquehanna, some north as far as Great Island. Mr. Porter, who has just demonstrated the power of the Scotch-Irishman to write poetry, is a Huntingdon County man.

When I told them in Lexington that the first President of Washington-Lee University was born in Dauphin County, graduated from Princeton, and then studied theology under John Roan, one of the first Presbyterian preachers of the Paxtang Valley, many of them seemed not to know that fact in the history of the first President of Washington-Lee University. And furthermore, that the first man—the first minister—who preached the Gospel in the great Valley of Virginia was James Anderson, who went from Old Donegal, and while I know you have not forgotten the birthplace of your ancestors, I would most earnestly invite you to make the meeting of the Scotch-Irish Congress an occasion for revisiting it.

Let me urge you, then, to come back to your birthplace and the birthplace of many of your ancestors to help us celebrate the glories of the Scotch-Irish race. We want you to come home. We shall endeavor to make it interesting to you.

The President :—

Well, we will all resolve to try to get to Harrisburg. That resolution will be seconded by a gentleman who hails from the Cumberland Valley, a beautiful and historic section, settled by our ancestral stock and still chock full of their descendants. We will hear from State Senator McCarrol.

Hon. S. J. M. McCarrol :—

Mr. President:—The late lamented Thomas Nelson, who came from County Tyrone to Philadelphia in 1783, had very greatly the advantage of myself at this time. In one of the graveyards of County Tyrone there stands to-day a tombstone with this inscription :—

> "Here lie the remains of Thomas Nelson,
> Who emigrated to Philadelphia in 1783.
> If he had lived he would have been buried here."

(Laughter.) Mr. Nelson evidently had notice from his friends in Tyrone that they intended to lay violent hands upon him and precipitate his early burial, and therefore he emigrated to Philadelphia with great promptness. If I had received a like notice yesterday I think I should have revised the song to which we listened with so much pleasure this evening, and have sung, "I'll get out of Philadelphia in the Mornin'."

Some years ago a traveler stood in the beautiful Prince's Gardens at Edinburgh, looking at the monument erected to the memory of Walter Scott. As he was admiring its beautiful proportions a little newsboy came along, and the stranger said to him, "My boy, whose monument is this?" The little fellow said, "That is Sir Walter Scott's." "And what did he do, my little man, that led his countrymen to build this monument for him?" The little fellow, not being very well versed in the history of Sir Walter Scott, said, after a moment's hesitation, "He deed (died), sir." The little fellow was not right. He did not state the true reason which led to the erection of that beautiful monument to Sir Walter. He had forgotten that in his life Sir Walter had touched the hearts of his fellow men in such a way as to lead them, when he died, to raise that testimonial of their esteem and respect for him. And so we are here to-night to talk of our ancestors, not because they died, but because of the glory of their lives; because in their life they touched, and helped, and influenced, and lifted up their fellow men, and helped to make this great American nation what it is to-day.

I was greatly interested in listening, a few moments ago, to what was said of the condition of our countrymen on the other side, and the battle they are making for human rights. I listened with great interest to the reference which was made to that which has transpired on the banks of the Boyne. There is another circumstance in which I know you will be interested. It was my privilege, a little more than a year ago, to be in the city of Dublin. I visited what was once the Capitol of old Ireland, when she had her place among the nations of the earth; and I sat in what was the House of Lords in that day. The Houses of Parliament—the Capitol building—are occupied to-day by the Bank of Ireland. That which was the House of Lords is now the Directors' room of the Bank of Ireland; and it was a gratifying thing to me, a Scotch-Irishman, to find that Scotch-Irish still control and assert an influence that is potent in the city of Dublin, because upon the one side of that which was once the House of Lords there hung a tapestry portraying the deeds of the apprentice boys at Londonderry (applause), and on the other side there was a tapestry depicting William of Orange and his forces at the battle of the Boyne. That, in the city of Dublin, in good old Ireland, shows the influence which Scotch-Irishmen are exerting to-day for the principles for which the apprentice boys contended and for which William of Orange fought and won the victory at the battle of the Boyne. It is a matter of gratification, and we are all proud to-night of the fact, that upon every battlefield in this land, from Bunker Hill to Appomattox, the voices of the apprentice boys who fought at Londonderry, transmitted from generation to generation, rang out loud and clear above the din and conflict of the strife; and in every struggle for liberty in this good land the same spirit which fired the hearts and nerved the arms of the men who stood with William at the battle of the Boyne has controlled and actuated and won victories for the cause of liberty. They have won much, they have done much for the cause of humanity. Let us, by our lives, touch, and help, and lift up, and influence for good the lives of our fellow men. Thus shall we make America what she is destined to be among the nations of the world; thus shall we make it the home of the free, the land of liberty, the land where justice and right are recognized, and where the doctrines of individual right and of individual responsibility shall be asserted and maintained and recognized by all.

Now, I hope you will all come up to Harrisburg to attend the meeting of the American Congress in May. My brother McAlarney, who came over from Blarney, will be there with welcome as sweet as ever Kate Karney gave to those who visited Killarney and the beautiful lakes.

The Apollo Quartette then sang "Oh, Susanna."

The President :—

We have with us to-night representatives of our sister clubs or societies. I am sure the pilgrims from Ulster, while they have a due appreciation of their own importance, not only individually, but relatively to the country and the world at large, are not so narrow as to deny or in any way belittle the work which has been wrought by those of other races. Among those who have been most closely allied with us, and who have had a great many, and who still have a great many common characteristics with us, are the Pilgrims of New England. We are glad to have their representative here to-night, and to have him speak a few words of greeting to us, representing the Society of which he is the honored President. I need hardly name him. There is no nobler name in this city of noble men and women, this city of Philadelphia of which we are justly so proud, than the name of John H. Converse, President of the New England Society. (Applause.)

Mr. J. H. Converse :—

MR. PRESIDENT AND GENTLEMEN OF THE SCOTCH-IRISH SO-CIETY :—It is only a few weeks ago that you, Mr. President, did the New England Society the honor of filling, and filling most nobly, what otherwise would have been an aching void in our programme. You amiably criticised me for calling upon you forty-eight hours before the meeting, and not only inform-ing you that you were expected to make a speech, but being so impertinent as to dictate the subject. But nobly did you discharge your duty. This, I suppose, is a species of retalia-tion. I, however, thank you for the compliment that you convey to me personally, and I thank you for it as a recogni-tion of the New England Society. I cannot adequately re-spond, for " I am no orator as Brutus is." But, Mr. President, I must acknowledge the great interest which I feel in a gath-ering of this kind. It arouses my sympathies, it increases my appreciation, it enlarges my knowledge. I learn much which I trust will be of use to me in the future. I am particularly struck by the overwhelming modesty of the Scotch-Irish So-ciety. I am especially impressed by the entire absence of any reference to ancestry, to heroic achievement, or to the part which your lineage is to bear in the future development of the country. Some of you whom we have had the pleasure of entertaining at our hospitable board (and I hope you may so call it) have noticed quite the reverse in our attitude. Al-though the Pilgrim Fathers are not often alluded to, and the term " Yankee" is only occasionally used, it is true we do sometimes say something about the Pilgrim Mothers. I re-member that one of our speakers very appropriately remarked that they deserved more credit than the Fathers, for whilst they had to bear all the hardships which the Pilgrim Fathers had to bear, they had to bear the Pilgrim Fathers also. (Ap-plause.)

Mr. President, I confess I feel to-night a great deal of em-barrassment in sitting under your administration, for you occupy a very peculiar position—I think I might call you a sort of a triple alliance, perhaps a tripartite entity—you claim to be Irish and you claim to be Scotch, and we have made up our minds that before another festival of the New England Society takes place you shall be enrolled as a New Englander, for we concede that you are abundantly entitled to it.

The embarrassment that I have in speaking to-night, which is a natural one, is the profound ignorance of what I am expected to speak about. I am not quite certain whether it is Scotch or Irish which is wanted most.

I remember in a play I saw in London that "Walker," who is a guest on a house boat on the Thames, finding that the maid servant is going to the city to get supplies for the family, mysteriously whispers a commission which he wishes to have her execute. It is admirably done, and none of the guests have an idea what that mysterious commission is ; but a Hibernian servant is she, and as she leaves the room she turns and asks, " Scotch or Irish ? " (Laughter.)

But, Mr. President, I suppose that all of these organizations are very much alike. Our object is to honor a worthy ancestry. If we haven't any ancestors of our own we will adopt them ; we will be our own ancestors, if it is necessary. I had the satisfaction of hearing from my good friend, the ex-Mayor, a few moments ago, a little story which perhaps illustrates the position of these Societies. We are all pretty much alike ; we are all in the same box. During the recent troubles of the Traction Company in Philadelphia, of which I presume some of you may have heard, and some of you who have had to wear out shoe leather in walking up and down the streets during that slight unpleasantness may remember, a new conductor was placed in charge of a car. I have no doubt he was a member of this Society, for I believe he was a full-blooded Irishman. As he went into the car to collect the fares he found a number of turbulent people there who had no disposition to pay in the prevailing state of uneasiness. He tapped one man on the shoulder and said, " Your fare, sir." The man said, " What do you take me for ? " The conductor answered, " I take you for five cents, the same as everybody else." (Applause.)

The President :—

The President of the New England Society has disclaimed ability to speak eloquently, but having now heard him he will permit us to insist, at least, that he does *converse* mighty well. (Laughter and applause.)

We are drawing very close to the time when we ought to go home ; when we want to go home, anyhow. But before we separate we ought to hear from the Dinner Committee, which has served us so admirably. No one has been more efficient in that service than Mr. James Pollock. You recognize the name—whether James Pollock, of Philadelphia, or General and Bishop Polk, of the Confederate army, or James K. Polk, President of the United States, they are all of the same old Scotch stock—by way of Ulster. Shall we hear a word from Mr. Pollock ?

Mr. Pollock :—

MR. PRESIDENT:—While I thank you for your kindness in calling upon me at this late hour, I regret that my limited abilities will not permit me to reply in fitting terms to a subject that I know so little about. I find myself in the condition of the owner of some of the land in Ireland that our friend Dr. Munro was telling us about. The man happened to be slightly deaf, and was sitting upon the stone fence that inclosed a part of his farm, when a traveler approached him and asked him in a low tone of voice what kind of land this was. Not getting a reply he drew closer and asked him what he raised on this land. He replied to him, in a whisper, " My friend, nothing. I cannot even raise my voice upon this land." So it is with me. After the very able speeches that have been made to-night upon the subject of the Scotch-Irish I cannot raise my voice, but will defer my speech to a time when the members of this Society will be in a condition to appreciate a good speech when they hear it.

The President :—

If Mr. Pollock does not appreciate the feast, or has not appreciated the speeches, we certainly have appreciated the dinner, and we are thankful to him for his services in providing it.

Now it is possible that before you go some of you would like to hear some more of these songs. "Old Black Joe" has been asked for. "Old Black Joe" was the last of the negro melodies that Mr. Foster wrote.

The Apollo Quartette then sang "Old Black Joe."

The President :—

I ask your attention one moment to a word from Mr. Porter suggesting a matter that will meet the hearty response of all present.

Mr. W. W. Porter :—

MR. CHAIRMAN AND GENTLEMEN :—We have had to-night a jovial meeting, and there have been some features of it which were extremely solemnizing. We have lost our Secretary, and we have recently lost a prominent member in Judge Allison. There was another member of this Society, a man who had identified himself with some of the greatest enterprises of the State of Pennsylvania, whose name was known, not only throughout this State, but throughout the broad land; a man who was as kindly at heart as he was great in mind; a man who was as quiet in his charities as he was in many of his other great deeds. This man has been taken from us, and I think it only proper that we should, at this time, enter upon our records some notice of the death of Henry H. Houston. I therefore ask that a proper minute be made of his death.

It was directed that the same gentlemen appointed to draft a minute as to Hon. Judge Allison should prepare a memorial as to Mr. Houston.

The President :—

Gentlemen, is there any other song you would like to have sung? Will you wait for another? No. 5 has been asked for before we separate—"Hard Times Come Again no More."

The Apollo Quartette then sang "Hard Times."

The President :—

Now, gentlemen, your Chairman has endeavored to carry out as best he could the order committed to him by your learned and efficient Council. I am sure that most of us have had a pretty good time—I may say all except those who have had to make speeches, and their good time did not begin until their speeches were safely over. I would like, before we go, to emphasize what our temporary Secretary has spoken regarding the increase of this Society. We have only about two hundred members. We have been extremely "select" in selecting our members. We do not wish to be any less select in choosing, but a little more diligent in obtaining. I am sure there is not a member here to-night who could not send to the Council for election half a hundred names of influential men. We want to have next year's banquet spread for at least two hundred guests. Shall not we have it so ? You have the material from which to choose, abundant and the very best, in all walks of life. If you men will see to it that a few of these are "corraled" for this Society there is not a doubt that you will succeed. I thank you most heartily for what you have done to-night to make this meeting a success.

Mr. Richardson L. Wright :—

MR. PRESIDENT :—Before we disperse I think there is something in the way of a tribute due to the retiring President of this Society. We have all been so much pleased at the evidence of his remarkable skill in managing a dinner such as we have had to-night, and in bringing to our notice and to our hearing so many good speakers, that I think some recognition of what he has done should be manifested by us. I therefore move that a vote of thanks be tendered the retiring President for the able and skillful manner in which he has managed the affairs of this Society.

The motion was unanimously carried.

The President :—

Gentlemen, I thank you. I was upon the point—indeed the gentleman took the words out of my mouth—of returning thanks to those who have so ably helped in the conduct of this dinner, and who, far more than your President, have made it a success under adverse circumstances. It shows what the Scotch-Irish can do when they put their minds upon a matter. There is an old proverb of our ancestors, " Praise the fair day at aven'." Your Council did not feel this morning like praising the day, for in sooth it was sorely beclouded, but now that "the aven'" is over I think we can sincerely sing the long metre Doxology, and it is time for it ; but as this is not an ecclesiastical event, perhaps instead of that we may sing " Auld Lang Syne."

All present arose and sang " Auld Lang Syne."

CONSTITUTION AND BY-LAWS.

———⊕———

I. Name.

The name of the Association shall be the "Pennsylvania Scotch-Irish Society," and it shall constitute the Pennsylvania branch of the Scotch-Irish Society of America.

II. Objects.

The purposes of this Society are the preservation of Scotch-Irish history; the keeping alive the *esprit de corps* of the race; and the promotion of social intercourse and fraternal feeling among its members, now and hereafter.

III. Membership.

1. Any male person of good character, at least twenty-one years of age, residing in the State of Pennsylvania, of Scotch-Irish descent through one or both parents, shall be eligible to membership, and shall become a member by the majority vote of the Society or of its Council, subscribing these articles, and paying an annual fee of two dollars: *Provided*, That all persons whose names were enrolled prior to February 13th, 1890, are members: *And provided further*, That three officers of the National Society, to be named by it, shall be admitted to sit and deliberate with this Society.

2. The Society, by a two-thirds vote of its members present at any regular meeting, may suspend from the privileges of the Society, or remove altogether, any person guilty of gross misconduct.

3. Any member who shall have failed to pay his dues for two consecutive years, without giving reasons satisfactory to the Council, shall, after thirty days' notice of such failure, be dropped from the roll.

IV. Annual Meeting.

1. The annual meeting shall be held at such time and place as shall be determined by the Council. Notice of the same shall be given in the Philadelphia daily papers, and be mailed to each member of the Society.

2. Special meetings may be called by the President or a Vice-President, or, in their absence, by two members of the Council.

V. Officers and Committees.

At each annual meeting there shall be elected a President, a First and Second Vice-President, a Treasurer, a Secretary, and twelve Directors, but the same person may be both Secretary and Treasurer.

They shall enter upon office on the 1st of March next succeeding, and shall serve for one year and until their successors are chosen. The officers and Directors together with the ex-Presidents of the Society shall constitute the Council. Of the Council there shall be four Standing Committees.

1. On admission; consisting of four Directors, the Secretary, and the First Vice-President.

2. On Finance; consisting of the officers of the Society.

3. On Entertainments; consisting of the Second Vice-President and four Directors.

4. On History and Archives; consisting of four Directors.

VI. Duties of Officers.

1. The President, or in his absence the First Vice-President, or if he too is absent the Second Vice-President, shall preside at all meetings of the Society or the Council. In the absence at any time of all these, then a temporary Chairman shall be chosen.

2. The Secretary shall keep a record of the proceedings of the Society and of the Council.

3. The Treasurer shall have charge of all moneys and securities of the Society; he shall, under the direction of the Finance Committee, pay all its bills, and at the meeting of

said committee next preceding the annual meeting of the Society shall make a full and detailed report.

VII. Duties of Committees.

1. The Committee on Admission shall consider and report, to the Council or to the Society, upon all names of persons submitted for membership.

2. The Finance Committee shall audit all claims against the Society, and, through a sub-committee, shall audit annually the accounts of the Treasurer.

3. The Committee on Entertainments shall, under the direction of the Council, provide for the annual banquet.

4. The Committee on History and Archives shall provide for the collection and preservation of the history and records of the achievements of the Scotch-Irish people of America, and especially of Pennsylvania.

VIII. Changes.

The Council may enlarge or diminish the duties and powers of the officers and committees at its pleasure, and fill vacancies occurring during the year by death or resignation.

IX. Quorum.

Fifteen members shall constitute a quorum of the Society; of the Council five members, and of the committees a majority.

X. Fees.

The annual dues shall be two dollars, and shall be payable on February 1st in each year.

XI. Banquet.

The annual banquet of the Society shall be held on the second Thursday of February, at such time and in such manner, and such other day and place, as shall be determined by the Council. The costs of the same shall be at the charge of those attending it.

XII. AMENDMENTS.

1. These articles may be altered or amended at any annual meeting of the Society, the proposed amendment having been approved by the Council, and notice of such proposed amendment sent to each member with the notice of the annual meeting.

2. They may also be amended at any meeting of the Society, provided that the alteration shall have been submitted at a previous meeting.

3. No amendment or alteration shall be made without the approval of two-thirds of the members present at the time of their final consideration, and not less than twenty-five voters for such alteration or amendment.

APPENDIX A.

———⊕———

REPORT OF WILLIAM RIGHTER FISHER, TEMPORARY TREASURER
PENNSYLVANIA SCOTCH-IRISH SOCIETY, MADE FEBRUARY 13TH,
1896.

1896.   DR.

Feb. 1—Balance from last year $622 59
  Sale of Proceedings, 1890-4 . . . .   18 00
  Interest on deposit 15 05
  Dues for 1895 and subscriptions to sixth annual
    dinner 456 00
                                                           _____
                                                            $1111 64

CR.

  Hotel Bellevue, sixth dinner $369 20
  Allen, Lane & Scott, printing 116 75
  Stenographer and clerk hire 40 00
  Menus 23 00
  Music 15 00
  Hoskins for invitations 14 25
  J. L. H. Bayne, binding Proceedings 1890-4,   11 61
  Postage, stationery, &c. 14 44
                                              _____
                                               $604 25
  Balance 507 39
                                              ———— $1111 64
                                                           =========

WM. RIGHTER FISHER,
Treasurer.

(67)

LIST OF MEMBERS.

ALEXANDER ADAMS . . . . . . 1621 Derry St., Harrisburg, Pa.
W. J. ADAMS . . . . Harrisburg, Pa.
HON. J. SIMPSON AFRICA . . . Union Trust Co., 719 Chestnut St., Phila.
HON. DANIEL AGNEW . . . . . Beaver, Beaver County, Pa.
HON. WILLIAM H. ARMSTRONG, Continental Hotel, Philadelphia.
JAMES M. BARNETT . . . . . . New Bloomfield, Perry County, Pa.
JOHN CROMWELL BELL . . . . 1001 Chestnut St., Philadelphia.
R. T. BLACK . . . . Scranton, Pa.
J. C. BLAIR . . . . Huntingdon, Pa.
P. P. BOWLES . . . . 4041 Chestnut Street, Philadelphia.
SAMUEL BRADBURY . . . . . Wayne Ave., Germantown, Phila.
SAMUEL R. BROADBENT . . . . 3431 Walnut St., Philadelphia.
JOHN W. BUCHANAN . . . . . Beaver, Beaver County, Pa.
REV. C. W. BUOY, D. D. . . . 1334 Arch St., Philadelphia.
CHARLES ELMER BUSHNELL . . S. E. cor. 4th and Chestnut Sts., Phila.
W. J. CALDER . . . . 5 South Second St., Harrisburg, Pa.
J. ALBERT CALDWELL . . . . . 902 Chestnut St., Philadelphia.
SETH CALDWELL, JR. . . . . . 1939 Chestnut St. (Girard Bank, Third
                                below Chestnut), Philadelphia.
HON. J. DONALD CAMERON . . U. S. Senate, Washington, D. C.
HON. EDWARD CAMPBELL . . . Uniontown, Fayette County, Pa.
GEORGE CAMPBELL . . . . . . Washington Ave. and 21st St., Phila.
GEORGE CAMPBELL . . . . . . Hotel Hamilton, Philadelphia.
HON. J. D. CAMPBELL . . . . P. & R. Terminal, Philadelphia.
ROBERT CARSON . . . . Huntingdon St. and Trenton Ave., Phila.
HENRY CARVER . . . . Harrison Building, Philadelphia.
A. J. CASSATT . . . . Haverford, Pa.
COL. JOHN CASSELS . . . . . 1907 F St., Washington, D. C.
REV. WILLIAM CATHCART, D. D., Hoyt, Montgomery County, Pa.
JOHN H. CHESTNUT . . . . . . 636 Drexel Building, Philadelphia.
JOHN H. W. CHESTNUT, M. D. . 1757 Frankford Ave., Philadelphia.
A. H. CHRISTY . . . . Scranton, Pa.
JAMES CLARK . . . . Harrisburg, Pa.
ROWAN CLARK, M. D. . . . . 112 Logan St., Tyrone, Pa.
CHARLES H. CLARKE . . . . . 3943 Market St., Philadelphia.
THOMAS COCHRAN . . . . . . 4200 Walnut St., Philadelphia.
REV. DAVID CONWAY . . . . Mount Joy, Lancaster County, Pa.
REV. J. AGNEW CRAWFORD, D. D., Chambersburg, Pa.
ALEXANDER CROW, JR. . . . . 2112 Spring Garden St., Philadelphia.
ROLAND G. CURTIN, M. D. . . 22 South Eighteenth St., Philadelphia.

Hon. John Dalzell . . . . . House of Representatives, Washington, D. C.
E. B. Dawson . . . . Uniontown, Fayette County, Pa.
John B. Deaver, M. D. . . . 120 S. Eighteenth St., Philadelphia.
James Aylward Develin . . 400 Chestnut St., Phila., Wood Building.
Rev. Charles A. Dickey, D. D., 2211 St. James Place, Philadelphia.
J. M. C. Dickey . . . . . . Oxford, Chester County, Pa.
S. Ralston Dickey . . . . . Oxford, Chester County, Pa.
A. W. Dickson . . . . . . Scranton, Pa.
James P. Dickson . . . . . Scranton, Pa.
Dr. James L. Diven . . . . New Bloomfield, Perry County, Pa.
J. P. Donaldson . . . . . . Manhattan Life Building, Fourth and Walnut Sts., Philadelphia.
Robert Dornan . . . . . . Howard, Oxford, and Mascher Sts., Phila.
Rev. Geo. S. Duncan, Ph. D. . 1208 N. Second St., Harrisburg, Pa.
Daniel M. Easter, M. D. . . . 1516 Christian St., Philadelphia.
Hon. T. B. Elder . . . . . . Elders' Ridge, Indiana County, Pa.
Rev. Alfred L. Elwyn . . . 1422 Walnut St., Philadelphia.
Rev. Ebenezer Erskine, D. D., Newville, Cumberland County, Pa.
Hon. Nathaniel Ewing . . . Uniontown, Fayette County, Pa.
Hon. Thomas Ewing . . . . Pittsburgh, Pa.
Samuel Evans . . . . Columbia, Pa.
Edgar Dudley Faries . . . . 308 Walnut St., Philadelphia.
Hon. Joseph C. Ferguson . . 1423 North Broad St., Philadelphia.
William N. Ferguson, M. D. . 116 West York St., Philadelphia.
John Field . . . . Young, Smyth, Field & Co., 816 Market St., Philadelphia.
William M. Field . . . . . . 1823 Spruce St., Philadelphia.
Hon. Thomas K. Finletter . 500 North Fifth St., Philadelphia.
William Righter Fisher . . 750 Drexel Building, Philadelphia.
D. Fleming . . . . 325 North Front St., Harrisburg, Pa.
Samuel W. Fleming . . . . . 32 North Third St., Harrisburg, Pa.
Hon. Morrison Foster . . . . Shields, Allegheny County, Pa.
Hugh R. Fulton . . . . . . Lancaster, Pa.
Rev. Robert H. Fulton, D. D., 3420 Hamilton St., Philadelphia.
Harvey Græme Furbie . . . The Lorraine, Broad and Fairmount Ave., Philadelphia.
Rev. S. A. Gayley . . . . . Wayne, Pa.
Rev. W. H. Gill, D. D. . . . 1318 South Broad St., Philadelphia.
Samuel F. Givin . . . . . . 2116 Chestnut St., Philadelphia.
William B. Givin . . . . . 204 Locust St., Columbia, Pa.
Hon. Jas. Gay Gordon . . . 1628 North Thirteenth St., Philadelphia.
Albert Graff . . . . 4048 Walnut St., Philadelphia.
Duncan M. Graham . . . . . Carlisle, Pa.
John Graham . . . . Wilkesbarre, Pa.
John H. Graham . . . . . . 533 Drexel Building, Philadelphia.
Rev. Loyal Y. Graham, D. D., 2325 Green St., Philadelphia.

Theodore R. Graham	1917 Wallace St., Philadelphia.
Capt. John P. Green	Pennsylvania Railroad Office, Broad and Market Sts., Philadelphia.
J. M. Guffy	43 Sixth Ave., Pittsburgh, Pa.
Hon. J. Milton Guthrie . . .	Indiana, Pa.
William Hammersly	Broad Street Station, Philadelphia.
Hon. William B. Hanna . .	110 South Thirty-eighth St., Philadelphia.
Capt. John C. Harvey . . .	Harrisburg, Pa.
Hon. Daniel H. Hastings . .	Harrisburg, Pa.
George Hay	25 South Water St., Philadelphia.
James Hay	25 South Water St., Philadelphia.
John Hays	Carlisle, Pa.
Rev. I. N. Hays, D. D. . . .	117 Sheffield St., Allegheny, Pa.
Rev. John Hemphill, D. D. .	2220 Spruce St., Philadelphia.
Hon. R. M. Henderson . . .	Carlisle, Cumberland County, Pa.
Charles W. Henry	Wissahickon Heights, Philadelphia.
J. Bayard Henry	701 Drexel Building, Philadelphia.
Col. W. A. Herron	80 Fourth Ave., Pittsburgh, Pa.
A. G. Hetherington	2049 Chestnut St., Philadelphia.
James W. Houston	27 Seventh Ave., Pittsburgh, Pa.
Jno. J. L. Houston	814 North Twenty-first St., Philadelphia.
Samuel F. Houston	308 Walnut St., Philadelphia.
Joseph M. Houston	Provident Building, Phila.
B. K. Jamison	137 South Fifth St., Philadelphia.
John W. Jordan	1300 Locust St., Philadelphia, Historical Society of Pennsylvania.
William J. Jordan	804 North Twentieth St., Philadelphia.
George Junkin	532 Walnut St., Philadelphia.
Joseph De F. Junkin	532 Walnut St., Philadelphia.
George C. Kennedy	38 North Duke St., Lancaster, Pa.
Col. Thos. B. Kennedy . . .	Chambersburg, Franklin Co., Pa.
Hon. James Kerr	
H. P. Laird	Greensburg, Pa.
Hon. James W. Latimer . . .	York, York County, Pa.
John S. Latta	1217 Market St., Philadelphia.
William J. Latta	Broad St. Station, Philadelphia.
Rev. Wm. Laurie, D.D. . . .	Bellefonte, Pa.
John A. Linn	Radnor, Pa.
Harry V. Logan, M.D. . . .	Scranton, Pa.
Hon. James A. Logan	Broad St. Station, P. R. R., Philadelphia.
John P. Logan	826 Drexel Building, Philadelphia.
Rev. Samuel C. Logan, D.D. .	Scranton, Pa.
Wm. P. Logan	826 Drexel Building, Philadelphia.
James Long	203 Church St., Philadelphia.
Rev. J. S. MacIntosh, D. D. .	1334 Chestnut St., Philadelphia.
Thomas MacKellar	612 Sansom St., Philadelphia.
James F. Magee	114 North Seventeenth St., Philadelphia

W. M. McAlarney . . . . . "The Telegraph," Harrisburg, Pa.
Hon. H. J. McAteer . . . . Alexandria, Huntingdon County, Pa.
Hon. Robert McCachran . . Newville, Cumberland County, Pa.
Hon. Samuel J. M. McCarrell, Harrisburg, Pa.
J. P. McCaskey . . . . . · . "Penna. School Journal," Lancaster, Pa.
Hon. William McLean . . . . Gettysburg, Adams County, Pa.
Alexander K. McClure . . . "The Times," Eighth and Chestnut Sts.,
　　　　　　　　　　　　　　 Philadelphia.
Justice J. Brewster McCollum, Girard House, Philadelphia.
R. S. McCombs, M. D. . . . . 648 North Eleventh St., Philadelphia.
Dr. William McCombs . . . . Hazleton, Pa.
Hon. A. D. McConnell . . . Greensburg, Pa.
Rev. S. D. McConnell, D.D. . 157 Montague St., Brooklyn.
Rev. Henry C. McCook, D.D., 3700 Chestnut St., Philadelphia.
John D. McCord . . . . . . 2004 Spruce St., Philadelphia.
Edward B. McCormick . . . Greensburg, Pa.
Hon. Henry C. McCormick . Harrisburg, Pa.
W. H. McCrea . . . . Carlisle, Pa.
George D. McCreary . . . . 3301 Arch St., Philadelphia.
M. Simpson McCullough . . . 1717 Spring Garden St., Philadelphia.
John C. McCurdy . . . . . . 2200 North Front St., Philadelphia.
Rev. O. B. McCurdy . . . . . Duncannon, Pa.
J. A. McDowell . . . . 1727 Walnut St., Philadelphia.
John M. McDowell . . . . . Chambersburg, Pa.
William H. McFadden, M. D., 3505 Hamilton St., Philadelphia.
John McIlhenny . . . . . . 1339 Cherry St., Philadelphia.
Dr. J. Atkinson McKee . . . 1628 Chestnut St., Philadelphia.
Charles L. McKeehan . . . 2116 Chestnut St., Philadelphia.
Dr. George I. McKelway . . 255 South Seventeenth St., Philadelphia.
George McKeown . . . . . . 506 Library St.,Phila.(care of F. H. Bailey).
Rev. H. W. McKnight . . . . Pennsylvania College, Gettysburg, Pa.
J. King McLanahan . . . . . Hollidaysburg, Pa.
Robert McMeen . . . . Mifflintown, Juniata County, Pa.
Hon. John B. McPherson . . Harrisburg, Pa.
Daniel N. McQuillen, M. D. . 1628 Chestnut St., Philadelphia.
Wm. F. McSparran . . . . . Furniss, Pa.
A. W. Mellon . . . . Pittsburgh, Pa.
Chas. H. Mellon . . . . . . 1734 Spruce St., Philadelphia.
Hon. Thomas Mellon . . . . Pittsburgh, Pa.
George Gluyas Mercer . . . 636 Drexel Building, Philadelphia.
John Houston Merrill . . . 625 Drexel Building, Philadelphia.
John S. Miller . . . . Harrisburg, Pa.
Rev. J. D. Moffat, D.D. . . . President of Washington and Jefferson
　　　　　　　　　　　　　　 College, Washington, Pa.
Robert H. Moffitt, D.D. . . 200 Pine St., Harrisburg, Pa.
Edward E. Montgomery, M. D., 1818 Arch St., Philadelphia.
Rev. J. H. Munro . . . . . . 714 North Broad St., Philadelphia.

S. A. Mutchmore	Eighteenth and Montgomery Ave., Phila.
H. S. P. Nichols	S. E. cor. Sixth and Walnut Sts., Phila.
A. Wilson Norris	No. 5 North Market Sq., Harrisburg, Pa.
H. M. North	Columbia, Lancaster County, Pa.
D. A. Orr	Harrisburg, Pa.
John G. Orr	Chambersburg, Pa.
William B. Orr	421 Wood St., Pittsburgh, Pa.
C. Stuart Patterson	600 Girard Building, Philadelphia.
D. Ramsey Patterson	525 Drexel Building, Philadelphia.
T. Elliott Patterson	501 Franklin Building, Philadelphia.
T. Hoge Patterson	1728 Spruce St., Philadelphia.
Theodore C. Patterson	715 Walnut St., Philadelphia.
Thomas Patterson	Carnegie Hall, Pittsburgh, Pa.
R. H. Patton	Roxborough, Pa.
Rev. W. A. Patton	Wayne, Delaware County, Pa.
Thomas R. Patton	1308 Pine St., Philadelphia.
William A. Patton	Broad St. Station, P. R. R., Philadelphia.
Rev. James D. Paxton, D. D.	2027 DeLancey Place, Philadelphia.
Hugh Pitcairn, M. D.	206 West State St., Harrisburg, Pa.
Robert Pitcairn	Supt. P. R. R. Co., Pittsburgh, Pa.
James Pollock	2226 East Dauphin St., Philadelphia.
Wm. W. Porter	623 Walnut St., Philadelphia.
William Potter	Stenton Avenue, Chestnut Hill, Phila.
Samuel Rea	Broad St. Station, P. R. R., Philadelphia.
R. S. Reed	Thirty-third and Chestnut Sts., Phila.
Prof. John Calvin Rice	Cheltenham Academy, Ogontz, Pa.
Hon. John B. Robinson	Media, Pa.
Rev. Thomas H. Robinson, D.D.,	Western Theological Seminary, Ridge Ave., Pittsburgh, Pa.
James Slocum Rogers	Fortieth and Spruce Sts., Philadelphia.
Talbot Mercer Rogers	Fortieth and Spruce Sts., Philadelphia.
J. E. Rutherford	Harrisburg, Pa.
W. F. Rutherford	P. O. Box 104, Harrisburg, Pa.
Charles Scott	1520 Arch St., Philadelphia.
Charles Scott, Jr.	Overbrook Farms, Philadelphia.
John Scott, Jr.	2218 Locust St., Philadelphia.
John B. Scott	1520 Arch St., Philadelphia.
William H. Scott	1211 Clover St., Philadelphia.
J. A. Searight	Uniontown, Pa.
T. B. Searight	Uniontown, Pa.
W. C. Shaw, M. D.	135 Wylie St., Pittsburgh, Pa.
Chas. T. Shoen	Hotel Stratford, Philadelphia.
Hon. J. W. Simonton	Harrisburg, Pa.
Rev. David M. Skilling	Harrisburg, Pa.
Chas. H. Smiley	New Bloomfield, Perry Co., Pa.
Frank W. Smith	134 South Twentieth St., Philadelphia.
Rev. S. E. Snively, M. D.	Sixty-third and Market Sts., Phila.

Hon. Robert Snodgrass . . . 13 North Third St., Harrisburg, Pa.
E. J. Stackpole . . . . Harrisburg, Pa.
Rev. William S. Steans . . . Washburn St., Scranton, Pa.
Rev. James D. Steele . . . . 29 West Ninety-third St., New York.
Justice James P. Sterrett . . 3800 Walnut St., Philadelphia.
George Stevenson . . . . . . 238 West Logan Square, Philadelphia.
George H. Stewart . . . . . Shippensburg, Pa.
Hon. John Stewart . . . . . Chambersburg, Franklin County, Pa.
Rev. George B. Stewart . . 215 North Second St., Harrisburg, Pa.
Samuel C. Stewart . . . . . 1429 Moravian St., Philadelphia.
William M. Stewart . . . . 2008 Walnut St., Philadelphia.
Hon. James A. Stranahan . . Mercer, Pa.
Hon. Edwin S. Stuart . . . . Philadelphia, Pa.
William Thompson . . . . . 233 South Thirty-ninth St., Philadelphia.
Dr. John A. Thomson . . . . Wrightsville, Pa.
Frank Thomson . . . . Broad St. Station, P. R. R., Philadelphia.
William Thomson, M. D. . . . 1426 Walnut St., Philadelphia.
Thomas L. Wallace . . . . . P. R. R. Freight Station, Harrisburg, Pa.
William S. Wallace . . . . 812 Girard Building, Philadelphia.
Rev. Frank T. Wheeler . . New Bloomfield, Perry County, Pa.
William Wigton . . . . . . New York City.
James S. Williams . . . . . . 711 Drexel Building, Philadelphia.
Justice Henry W. Williams . Continental Hotel, Philadelphia.
Prof. J. Clark Williams . . Pittsburgh, Pa.
Rev. David Wills . . . . . . Disston Memorial Church, Tacony, Pa.
Alexander Wilson, M. D. . . 1863 North Front St., Philadelphia.
M. J. Wilson, M. D. . . . . . 1750 Frankford Ave., Philadelphia.
Cyrus E. Woods . . . . Greensburg, Pa.
D. Walker Woods . . . . . Lewistown, Pa.
Hon. Joseph M. Woods . . . Lewistown, Pa.
Richard W. Woods . . . . . Carlisle, Pa.
John W. Woodside . . . . . 2107 Spring Garden St., Philadelphia.
Rev. Nevin Woodside . . . . 25 Granville St., Pittsburgh, Pa.
Hon. Richardson L. Wright . 4308 Frankford Ave., Philadelphia.
Hon. John Russell Young . . 2034 Arch St., Philadelphia.

In Memoriam.

C. Watson McKeehan.

For minute touching the death of Charles Watson Mc-
Keehan, late Secretary and Treasurer of the Society, see
page 27 of this report.

Hon. Joseph Allison.

The Hon. Joseph Allison was one of the original members
of this Society, and to those of Scotch-Irish descent his life
is a just source of ancestral gratification and pride. During
a career of more than forty years as a Judge of the Court
of Common Pleas, in the city and county of Philadelphia,
he illustrated in his life the happiest characteristics of the
sturdy race from which he sprang, and leaves a record of
arduous and often perplexing duties always well and benefi-
cently performed. He was at all times true to conscience,
impartial in the administration of justice, courteous towards
counsel and suitors, diligent in his search for the truth, and
vigorous and just in his application of the law. In all the
relations of life he ever manifested courage, fidelity to principle, a sterling love of truth, and great kindness of heart and
disposition. He was only intolerant of wrong and oppres-
sion, and of that viciousness of mind and heart which leads
to the degradation of mankind and the corruption of the
pure channels of human life and affection. Towards these
he displayed the irrepressible revulsion of a pure and benev-
olent nature. This Society lays upon his grave the chaplet
of sincere affection and esteem, and finds in the example of
his life a renewed impulse to faithful and upright living.

HENRY H. HOUSTON.

In the death of Henry H. Houston the Pennsylvania Scotch-Irish Society has lost one of its most honored and valued members. He was a man of singular simplicity of character, coupled with great largeness of heart and capaciousness of mental grasp. Busied during the whole of his mature manhood with enterprises of great moment in the industrial development of the State and involving large investments of individual capital, he displayed a practical common sense, an accuracy of judgment, a comprehensiveness of view, and an integrity of purpose which made him an invaluable aid to his associates and a potent factor in the promotion and management of the most important lines of transportation in the Commonwealth and nation. His successes were achieved without the sacrifice of uprightness and truth or the loss of human tenderness. The wealth which came to him as the just reward of well-directed industry and clearness of foresight was held in obedience to the Divine injunction of stewardship, and he was at all times the sympathetic, unostentatious friend of the helpless and unfortunate, and gave liberally of both time and money for the advancement of education, religion, and humanity. This Society here records its deep sense of loss in his decease and its high appreciation of his character and works, which will long remain as an inspiration and a blessing to his fellow men.

DECEASED MEMBERS.

Hon. Joseph Allison .... Philadelphia, Pa.

John Baird......................... Philadelphia, Pa.

Hon. Andrew G. Curtin.............. Bellefonte, Pa.

William Crossley................... Philadelphia, Pa.

William Holmes .... Pittsburgh, Pa.

H. H. Houston...................... Philadelphia, Pa.

Hon. R. A. Lamberton .... Harrisburg, Pa.

John Mundell .... Philadelphia, Pa.

C. Watson McKeehan .... Philadelphia, Pa.

James McKeehan .... Newville, Pa.

James E. McLean .... Shippensburg, Pa.

John P. Rutherford .... Harrisburg, Pa.

Hon. William A. Wallace........... Clearfield, Pa.

Hon. David Wills .... Gettysburg, Pa.

Col. John A. Wright................ Philadelphia, Pa.

www.ingramcontent.com/pod-product-compliance
Lightning Source LLC
Chambersburg PA
CBHW021420090426
42742CB00009B/1200